HOLY
INTERRUPTIONS

VOLUME 1
Rekindle

MIKEY OSBORNE

HOLY
INTERRUPTIONS

VOLUME 1
Rekindle

This is not just another devotional. This is not merely an intellectual walk through of the scriptures void of the vibrant relationship to which the Father has called us. May the words of this devotional and the Holy Scriptures come alive in you and lead you into an awakening. An awakening of your soul to the reality of being a son and daughter of the King and His Kingdom.

The devotionals in this compilation are driven to challenge you to interact with your Father in a real and authentic way. Some of the creative actions will challenge you, some of them will open hidden wounds in your heart but make room for the King with a spirit of repentance.

Break free from your inhibitions and enjoy the creative God by engaging with Him in an authentic, real, and personal way. Wholeheartedly devote yourself to meeting with the King through His word and praising Him with all your entire being.

DEDICATION

To all those who have participated and prepared creative worship stations during retreats over the years. Thank you for creativity, hard work, and dedication to the Gospel.

To Angie, Baylee, and Corbin for your encouragement, faithfulness, wit, humor, and patience.

To the Divine Wonder for all He has done, all He is doing, and those things yet to come.

HOW TO USE THIS DEVOTIONAL GUIDE

This is not your typical devotional; it was not fashioned for the casual reader. As you read through the pages of Rekindle, your heart, motivations, and sin will come to light. Commit yourself to the journey and allow the Holy Spirit to minister in ways mere words simply cannot.

Don't
*rush through each day
*value the creativity of the Engage portion of this devotional over His word

Do
*set aside a specific time and guard it as much as possible
*choose a place as free from distractions as possible
*be as authentic, vulnerable, and genuine before the Lord as possible
*complete the entire 40-day journey

For you…

May the Father divinely perform surgery upon every foundation of your life. May you encounter the Glorious King as you engage with His word. May your darkest sins be exposed, and loudest praises be lifted. And may your life be radically awakened to the incredible glory of our Savior.

DAY 1

*"in the church we seem to have lost the vision of
the majesty of God"*

\- JOHN STOTT

To the angel of the church in Ephesus write:

These are the words of him who holds the seven stars in his right hand and walks among the seven golden lampstands. I know your deeds, your hard work and your perseverance. I know that you cannot tolerate wicked people, that you have tested those who claim to be apostles but are not, and have found them false. You have persevered and have endured hardships for my name, and have not grown weary. Yet I hold this against you: You have forsaken the love you had at first.

\- Revelation 2:1-4

Read Revelation 2:1-4

For the church in Ephesus this was a shocking and utterly devastating statement. The entire body appeared to have everything together, when in fact, they were far from the Lord. Great revivals had occurred within the walls of this town. Paul spent his longest tenure with a Christian community here, yet the rebuke of the Lord is one of the harshest in the scriptures. They, the great Ephesus, the great place of revival, the very community that Paul himself taught; this thriving revival location had lost their first love.

How could this happen?

How could they leave the One that left heaven for them?

This is not an isolated event in history. The Israelites after watching the Red Sea drown their enemies willfully choose to turn to false gods. Saul after being empowered to defeat nations, ignores the divine regulations to honor God. Time and time again we observe the people of God falling into a dreadful state of apathy.

I don't know how it happens, but we too often creep into the same ghastly state. God's grace, which once sent us to our knees weeping in joy and disbelief, somehow devastatingly becomes common. Forgiveness, which use to flow freely from a forgiven heart, is rigorously withheld from others. And we slowly find ourselves having lost awe of our incredible grace-giving, all-powerful God.

> ### *Awe cannibalizes apathy!*

A son or daughter of the King cannot be in awe of God while simultaneously ignoring the majesty of the One he/she serves. IT. IS. Impossible.

Reflect:

When was the last time you were in awe of God's creation?

When was the last time you gazed upon the incredible attributes (power and Majesty) of our King?

The angels circling the throne of God never find themselves in want of anything to declare Holy, Holy, Holy. If you have lost your awe, the problem isn't the Father, it lies within the foundations of your very own heart. You've grown cold, numb to that which should continually amaze.

Engage:

Grab a piece of ice and hold it in your hand. Ask the Father to reveal the areas of your heart which have grown cold towards Him. Let the ice begin to melt. As it does, plead to the Father asking Him to restore the love you once had. Ask the Divine Wonder to restore your love for Him. Rejoice in His mercy and His love.

Notes:

DAY 2

"We must lay before Him what is in us, not what ought to be in us"

- C.S. LEWIS

My dear children, I write this to you so that you will not sin. But if anybody does sin, we have an advocate with the Father—Jesus Christ, the Righteous One.

- 1 John 2:1

For I am convinced that neither death nor life, neither angels nor demons, neither the present nor the future, nor any powers, neither height nor depth, nor anything else in all creation, will be able to separate us from the love of God that is in Christ Jesus our Lord.

- Romans 8:38-39

Whoever conceals their sins does not prosper, but the one who confesses and renounces them finds mercy.

- Proverbs 28:13

Read 1 John 2:1, Romans 8:38-3, Proverbs 28:13

It starts when we are young. We do not want to get in trouble, so we try to make up stories to cover our sin. We say we didn't eat the cookies, while chocolate chips gleam between the cracks in our teeth. With every word, we try to sweep our "dirt" under the rug. For some reason, we think we are better off hiding our shortcomings rather than letting everyone know.

As we get older, we somehow perfect this dreadful process. We learn how to sweep more efficiently, more effectively, and more convincingly. But no matter how much we perfect the process, we still hide things. We value the eyes of men more than the eyes of God. We continuously sweep things under the rug until we wake up one day and stumble over a HUGE mountain of sin under the upholstery.

And think of the incredible energy we use to conceal our sin. Our minds meditate on what we can say, how we can do it, and why we should continue indulging in the same things. We go to great physical and emotional lengths to make sure what we struggle with in private does not get publicly displayed. We continually sweep our "dirt" under the rug. Pretty soon, we feel guilty and find ourselves sliding downhill into awful places of loneliness, sin, and possibly even depression.

Concealment brings captivity!

If we confess our sins, He is faithful and just to forgive us our sins and to cleanse us from all unrighteousness (1 John 1:9).

The enemy will remind you of your sin; the Lord will give you victory over it. The enemy will slam you with guilt and shame; the Father will lift you with freedom and forgiveness. Spend sincere time in prayer asking the Lord to reveal the areas of your life you've hidden and confidently ask Him to exercise his gracious hand of mercy and extend forgiveness to you.

Reflect:

Do you have anything in your life you're hiding, something you've concealed in a futile effort thinking it might somehow magically disappear? Maybe you are concerned about the pain it might cause, the difficulty of the journey, or afraid it might tarnish the image you have so elegantly crafted. We often can't seem to overcome so we rigorously sweep it under the rug hoping no one, especially the Father, ever sees the obvious lump exposed in the room.

Engage:

Grab a bulky item from your house and place it under a rug to create a huge lump. Leave it there for the rest of the day and observe it. After placing it, approach God in prayer and ask Him to shine a light on areas of your life that you have been trying to hide. Now the option is yours, you can hold on to the "dirt" or ask the grace-giving Savior to liberate you. Spend time in prayer asking our gracious Father for forgiveness and then prayerfully remove the object from under the rug as a symbol of living in forgiveness instead of guilt.

Notes:

DAY 3

"Nothing binds me to my Lord like a strong belief in his changeless love"

- C.H. SPURGEON

What, then, shall we say in response to these things? If God is for us, who can be against us? He who did not spare his own Son, but gave him up for us all—how will he not also, along with him, graciously give us all things? Who will bring any charge against those whom God has chosen? It is God who justifies. Who then is the one who condemns? No one. Christ Jesus who died—more than that, who was raised to life—is at the right hand of God and is also interceding for us. Who shall separate us from the love of Christ? Shall trouble or hardship or persecution or famine or nakedness or danger or sword? As it is written:

"For your sake we face death all day long; we are considered as sheep to be slaughtered."

No, in all these things we are more than conquerors through him who loved us.

- Romans 8:31-37

Read Romans 8:31-37

What do you think God means when He said, "Nothing can separate you from the love of God…?"

Nothing means nothing. When the King of Kings declares there is nothing – then there is absolutely nothing. No sin, no lie, no enemy, no person, not even what you utter to yourself. There is an unimaginable confidence that ensues from knowing and understanding the great truths found in this promise from God.

God's love for you is unconditional. It is not based on your works, your moral successes, or anything else. It is hard for us to grasp this kind of love because so many of our relationships are based on our performance, our personality, or our ability to be something or someone.

> *You are loved.*
> *His love isn't fleeting or sporadic and will outlast time itself. His love literally lasts forever!*

This love isn't earned, it has been freely given. This Divine love is stamped with a promise from heaven and delivered by the obedience of Christ on the cross.

Spend some time letting this truth sink in. Take as long as you need.

Love this foreign is difficult to comprehend, but life-altering to receive.

Reread the passage and let the Father's love for you become a reality.

Reflect:

What do you often let rob you of the freedom of this truth?

What makes you think you are not loved?

Have you allowed the enemy to rob you of the blessing of being unconditionally loved by the King of Kings and the Lord of Lords?

Engage:

Spend time reflecting on the full lengths of the Father's love and the power He possesses to fully overcome anything which could threaten us from being separated from this amazing reality.

After a time of genuine reflection take out a pen and prayerfully craft a love letter back to the Father thanking Him for His overwhelming love and the power to keep His promises to His creation.

Notes:

DAY 4

"He's no failure. He's not dead yet"

- WILLIAM LLOYD GEORGE

but those who hope in the Lord
will renew their strength.
They will soar on wings like eagles;
they will run and not grow weary,
they will walk and not be faint.

- Isaiah 40:31

Read Isaiah 40:31

Have you ever felt tired? Unexplainably drained? Worn out? Dry? Weary? Frustrated to the point of wanting to give up?

In a boxing match two competitors go at each other brutally. The match, once it starts, can only end in one of four ways (1) Knock out (2) TKO – knock your opponent down three times (3) Judge's Decision - fight 10 full rounds and let the judges determine who wins or (4) one competitor gives up.

The fourth option isn't as foreign as one might think. Many times boxers "throw in the towel" and quit after going through several rounds of intense battle. Even after training for months – they cannot handle it anymore. These elite athletes are tired and worn out, so they abruptly stop. When a competitor embraces such a devastatingly grim state, they are told to throw the towel from their corner into the middle of the ring as a symbol of giving up. As such, we developed the terminology to "throw in the towel" and now apply it often to everyday life.

What about you?
What have you personally abandoned or deserted? A calling? A dream? A person?
Conquering a habitual sin? Consistency in your walk with God?
Hearing from God? Maturing in your faith?
Is there an area of your life where you feel like throwing in the towel... or maybe you already have?

> ***The best way out is still through.***

Reflect:

Ask God to identify areas of your life you have willfully abandoned.

Be honest with yourself. What have you given up on or thrown in the towel? What/Who have you forgotten, left behind, or deemed too difficult to continue to pursue? Use the Notes section to list out the things the Father reveals to you.

You may feel like the only one that has given up, but you are most certainly not alone.

Abraham loses faith in God and takes matters into his own hands…
Jonah doesn't just quit; he runs away…
Elijah felt abandoned so bad he asked God to take his life…
Peter is so distraught he denies he ever knew Christ…
In fact, many Christ followers, perhaps most, experience times when they want to throw in the towel.
This match isn't over, there's another round and you can do this with the Lord!

Engage:

Grab a household towel and throw it on the floor before you. Read the following words from the Lord slowly and let the Word encourage you: 2 Corinthians 4:8, 2 Corinthians 15:7, Galatians 6:9, Mark 10:27, Hebrews 12:1-3, Matthew 11:28

In light of His word, ask the Lord to renew your strength, to give you new fervor, to help you to not give up. Now prayerfully and purposefully pick up the towel as you ask the Lord to restore you fully.

Notes:

DAY 5

"Stagnation in the church is the devil's delight"

- C.H. SPURGEON

These are the words Moses spoke to all Israel in the wilderness east of the Jordan—that is, in the Arabah—opposite Suph, between Paran and Tophel, Laban, Hazeroth and Dizahab. (It takes eleven days to go from Horeb to Kadesh Barnea by the Mount Seir road.)

In the fortieth year, on the first day of the eleventh month, Moses proclaimed to the Israelites all that the Lord had commanded him concerning them. This was after he had defeated Sihon king of the Amorites, who reigned in Heshbon, and at Edrei had defeated Og king of Bashan, who reigned in Ashtaroth.

East of the Jordan in the territory of Moab, Moses began to expound this law, saying:

The Lord our God said to us at Horeb, "You have stayed long enough at this mountain. Break camp and advance into the hill country of the Amorites; go to all the neighboring peoples in the Arabah, in the mountains, in the western foothills, in the Negev and along the coast, to the land of the Canaanites and to Lebanon, as far as the great river, the Euphrates. See, I have given you this land. Go in and take possession of the land the Lord swore he would give to your fathers—to Abraham, Isaac and Jacob—and to their descendants after them."

- Deuteronomy 1:1-8

Read Deuteronomy 1:1-8

In this brief portion of scripture, Moses recounts all which has taken place during what has become known as the Exodus (the exiting of the Israelite people from slavery). When Moses talks about the journey, one thing becomes overwhelmingly evident: this should have been a lot shorter trip!

Most scholars believe the crossing should have taken only 11 days and instead this arduous journey took 40 years!

Can you imagine?

The laws of geometry teach us the shortest distance between two points is a straight line. Apparently, the Jewish people skipped class while enslaved in Egypt. They literally wandered in circles for 40 years instead of merely taking a brief journey for 11 days across the wilderness. In all honesty, this wasn't because of their lack of knowledge about geometry or even because they were lost. They did not progress because they were unwilling to embrace the lessons God sought to teach them, repeating the exact same mistakes time and time again.

As ridiculous as this sounds, many of us are guilty of going in circles spiritually. We fail to move forward, and instead camp out doing the same thing over and over and over and over and over again. What keeps circling back around in your own spiritual life? Like a rocking horse, there's plenty of movement, but no forward motion. Nothing can be more discouraging at times than a fixed state.

Stagnation is a breeding ground for apathy.

Reflect:

Is there a habitual sin lurking in the darkness that appears to be stuck on repeat in the soundtrack of your life?

Do you recurrently display a lack of faith or dependance on the Divine Wonder?

Where do you find yourself consistently abandoning your walk with God?

Have you exchanged your heavenly journey for a circular pattern of busyness? What busyness has taken priority over King Jesus?

Is there a continual repetition of disbelief, inconsistency, sinfulness, or prayerlessness that defines your interaction with our holy God?

Engage:

Go outside or in the largest room of your house and walk in the shape of a circle multiple times. Prayerfully walk the path and ask the Lord to reveal the areas of your life where you continue to camp out instead of moving forward.

Spend some time confessing your "circling path" in prayer to God. Willfully embrace and admit the areas of your life that continually surface time and time again which keep you from getting closer to God. Ask the Father to help you move forward, to learn what has continually escaped you, and to embrace the freedoms and victory He has given you.

Notes:

DAY 6

*"The greatest single distinguishing feature of the omnipotence
of God is that our imagination gets lost thinking about it"*

- BLAISE PASCAL

A man in the crowd answered, "Teacher, I brought you my son, who is possessed by a spirit that has robbed him of speech. Whenever it seizes him, it throws him to the ground. He foams at the mouth, gnashes his teeth and becomes rigid. I asked your disciples to drive out the spirit, but they could not."

"You unbelieving generation," Jesus replied, "how long shall I stay with you? How long shall I put up with you? Bring the boy to me."

So they brought him. When the spirit saw Jesus, it immediately threw the boy into a convulsion. He fell to the ground and rolled around, foaming at the mouth.

Jesus asked the boy's father, "How long has he been like this?"

"From childhood," he answered. "It has often thrown him into fire or water to kill him. But if you can do anything, take pity on us and help us."

"'If you can'?" said Jesus. "Everything is possible for one who believes."

Immediately the boy's father exclaimed, "I do believe; help me overcome my unbelief!"

- Mark 9:17-24

Read Mark 9:17-24

You cannot read the Bible without encountering story after story of people who were astonished, speechless, and often dumfounded by the overwhelming power of the Creator of the Universe. In fact, the most notable biblical narratives unfold as the Father impossibly performs a miracle, empowers the weak, or overcomes unbelievably perilous odds. The scriptures are littered with miraculous stories of God despite our constant tendency to walk in a state of disbelief. Think about it…

Massive armies are defeated without lifting a sword.
Seas part for those to walk over.
Food falls from heaven.
Men experience the brilliance of color as their blind eyes are opened.
Lame men get up and traverse crowded rooms without difficulty.

Believers had a ridiculously difficult time believing Paul was converted (Acts 9:20-22). They thought he was lying to imprison them for their own faith.

Those praying for Peter to be released from jail responded in disbelief when he knocked on their door while they were praying (Acts 12:15-17).

Jesus' own disciples questioned how he could feed the 5,000 with so little (John 6:5-9).

Reflect:

These stories are exciting to read and hear, but could God really do something similar within us? Through us? In those we love? In our communities?

If we were honest, many times we put our limitless, powerful, miracle-working God in a box when it comes to our life. These stories…they are good for us to read…good for us to talk about…but when it comes to God doing something similar in our life…well, we have a very difficult time believing it.

We have placed our limitless, unfathomable God inside a box we created out of unbelief, lack of faith, and a lack of understanding. This prison has tastelessly fashioned our lives into one not representative of a son or daughter of the Most-High King.

> *"My idea of God is not a divine idea. It has to be shattered*
> *time after time. He shatters it Himself."*
>
> *- C.S. LEWIS*

Limitations cower in the presence of the Almighty!

Engage:

Grab a box from a recent shipment or one laying around your house and write on it the numerous ways you have put the Almighty inside a box of limited ideas. Ask the Father to reveal areas which have unknowingly crept into your thoughts and everyday actions. Place the box in a place you will see it for the next week and constantly pray the Father will miraculously encounter each of the situations and help you overcome your disbelief.

Notes:

DAY 7

"You never lose the love of God. Guilt is the warning that temporarily you are out of touch"

- JACK DOMINIAN

Then seizing him, they led him away and took him into the house of the high priest. Peter followed at a distance. And when some there had kindled a fire in the middle of the courtyard and had sat down together, Peter sat down with them. A servant girl saw him seated there in the firelight. She looked closely at him and said, "This man was with him." But he denied it. "Woman, I don't know him," he said. A little later someone else saw him and said, "You also are one of them.""Man, I am not!" Peter replied.

About an hour later another asserted, "Certainly this fellow was with him, for he is a Galilean." Peter replied, "Man, I don't know what you're talking about!" Just as he was speaking, the rooster crowed. The Lord turned and looked straight at Peter. Then Peter remembered the word the Lord had spoken to him: "Before the rooster crows today, you will disown me three times." And he went outside and wept bitterly.

- Luke 22: 54-62

When they had finished eating, Jesus said to Simon Peter, "Simon son of John, do you love me more than these?" "Yes, Lord," he said, "you know that I love you."Jesus said, "Feed my lambs." Again Jesus said, "Simon son of John, do you love me?" He answered, "Yes, Lord, you know that I love you." Jesus said, "Take care of my sheep." The third time he said to him, "Simon son of John, do you love me?" Peter was hurt because Jesus asked him the third time, "Do you love me?" He said, "Lord, you know all things; you know that I love you." Jesus said, "Feed my sheep.

- John 21:15-17

Read Luke 22:54-62, John 21:15-17

Can you imagine the degradation and shame Peter experienced as he peered into the eyes of Jesus? Grief-stricken, Peter stood overjoyed in the presence of the risen Messiah as the reality of his denial formed the backdrop of their interaction. The memories of the past few days undoubtedly echoing through his mind like a roaring alarm time and time again. He was overjoyed, yet also full of shame.

Then the One Peter disowned repeatedly utters not once, not twice, but three times, "Peter do you love me?" Understandably so, the scriptures announced Peter was "grieved" or "overwhelmed" with sorrow when Jesus asked the third time. What would have been going through your mind if you stood there like Peter, entrenched in guilt, and drowning in regret? What would you have felt? Guilt? Shame? Would you be deliberating whether the King was about to reject you just as you rejected Him?

Thankfully our worst moments haven't been written down for all the world to read. We've all had times in which we have made huge mistakes, failed miserably, and/or just flat out sinned against our risen King. Like Peter, the guilt and shame that ensues after our failures has overtaken most of us. Painful as it may be, Paul breathes a word of encouragement in his letter to Corinth. Paul states there is a "godly sorrow that leads to repentance" (2 Cor. 7:10).

Conviction brings restoration, while guilt brings condemnation. Do not remain in the prison of regret. You can almost hear the lies of the enemy whispering in Peter's mind. "You messed up too bad this time! He'll never take you back! This is too big of a sin; you can't do anything with this; you are done!" Perhaps these words are tingling the ears of your life even now!

> *Guilt will leave you rotting in the waste of regret.*

Instead of rejection, Peter found restoration. Peter's three rejections were masterfully met with three statements for restoration!

Reflect:

Is there anything Christ has already freed you from to which you are bearing guilt? Past sins? Failed opportunities? Why do you continue to tightly grip the burden of guilt and shame? Have you allowed conviction to take root and lead you to repentance or are you still wallowing in guilt, shame, and self-pity?

Engage:

Grab a pencil and record areas of your life where you have been experiencing the burdensome pain of guilt. Look back over the list and present each one to the Lord through prayer. Confess and ask the God of Restoration to breathe life into each scenario that has haunted you for quite some time. As he does, joyfully erase the things you have listed. Joyfully thank Him in three different ways.

Notes:

DAY 8

The hand of the Lord was on me, and he brought me out by the Spirit of the Lord and set me in the middle of a valley; it was full of bones. He led me back and forth among them, and I saw a great many bones on the floor of the valley, bones that were very dry. He asked me, "Son of man, can these bones live?"

I said, "Sovereign Lord, you alone know."

Then he said to me, "Prophesy to these bones and say to them, 'Dry bones, hear the word of the Lord! This is what the Sovereign Lord says to these bones: I will make breath enter you, and you will come to life. I will attach tendons to you and make flesh come upon you and cover you with skin; I will put breath in you, and you will come to life. Then you will know that I am the Lord.'"

So I prophesied as I was commanded. And as I was prophesying, there was a noise, a rattling sound, and the bones came together, bone to bone. I looked, and tendons and flesh appeared on them and skin covered them, but there was no breath in them.

Then he said to me, "Prophesy to the breath; prophesy, son of man, and say to it, 'This is what the Sovereign Lord says: Come, breath, from the four winds and breathe into these slain, that they may live." So I prophesied as he commanded me, and breath entered them; they came to life and stood up on their feet—a vast army.

- Ezekiel 37:1-10

Read Ezekiel 37:1-10

This passage is one of the most graphic depictions in the entire Bible. What in the world was God trying to communicate to His people?

When this passage was written, Israel was in a dreadfully awful state. God's nation was without a king, without land, and without hope of restoration. Renewal seemed like a fairytale as they glanced around at the mountains of skeletal bones looming over their circumstances. Yet amid hopelessness, God speaks the unconscionable; there is, within this decaying picture, hope for life to spring forth.

Everything seemed to be against Israel, and slowly they embraced the vile lie; they were dead, and there was absolutely no chance for their renewal.

Like unburied skeletons, they were in a state of living death.
They had completely lost hope.
BUT…. The Father was not finished.

When the breath of God entered the bones, a picture of life, freedom, and power flowed out of what once reeked of death. Hope sprang forth like the morning dawn exposing the darkness. The impossibilities surrounding them suddenly embraced the power of the Most High!

Like Israel, many Christians have laid their hope to rest in the valley of death. Suddenly the sin one committed is too wretched for God to overcome. The opportunities wasted are too lost for God to recover. The relationships affected are too dysfunctional to be healthy again. To embrace such tragic thinking is not remotely Christian at all.

When the breath of God comes, things that are dead and powerless come to life!

No matter what the enemy has spoken over you or tried to destroy, do not be deceived… LIFE, ABUNDANT LIFE, can flow out of you through Jesus.

> ***God is not finished with you yet!***

There is a cadence within the Divine deposit inside of you stirring the rhythms of revival once again. And through Him, that which once teemed with life, can live again.

Reflect:

What about you? What is there in your life right now that appears to be in such a dreadful and horrible state? No chance for renewal? What is threatening the extinction of your hope? What is stirring you to believe there is absolutely NO HOPE, NO CHANCE for life, NO CHANCE for a change?

Engage:

You have a choice… you can continue to allow the enemy to fill you with lies and remain dormant or you can allow the breath of God to breathe life into your circumstances. You are not useless; your Christian walk is not dead – the Lord can restore you…RIGHT NOW! No matter what has happened, how dry your bones appear, how dead the bones are, God can bring them back to life. Write out a prayer over the dead parts of your life and ask the King to bring life to the bones the enemy has declared dead.

Notes:

DAY 9

"The world is suffering a neurosis of emptiness"

- CARL JUNG

So he came to a town in Samaria called Sychar, near the plot of ground Jacob had given to his son Joseph. Jacob's well was there, and Jesus, tired as he was from the journey, sat down by the well. It was about noon. When a Samaritan woman came to draw water, Jesus said to her, "Will you give me a drink?" (His disciples had gone into the town to buy food.) The Samaritan woman said to him, "You are a Jew and I am a Samaritan woman. How can you ask me for a drink?" (For Jews do not associate with Samaritans) Jesus answered her, "If you knew the gift of God and who it is that asks you for a drink, you would have asked him and he would have given you living water." "Sir," the woman said, "you have nothing to draw with and the well is deep. Where can you get this living water? Are you greater than our father Jacob, who gave us the well and drank from it himself, as did also his sons and his livestock?"

Jesus answered, "Everyone who drinks this water will be thirsty again, but whoever drinks the water I give them will never thirst. Indeed, the water I give them will become in them a spring of water welling up to eternal life." The woman said to him, "Sir, give me this water so that I won't get thirsty and have to keep coming here to draw water." He told her, "Go, call your husband and come back." "I have no husband," she replied. Jesus said to her, "You are right when you say you have no husband. The fact is, you have had five husbands, and the man you now have is not your husband. What you have just said is quite true." "Sir," the woman said, "I can see that you are a prophet. Our ancestors worshiped on this mountain, but you Jews claim that the place where we must worship is in Jerusalem."

31

"Woman," Jesus replied, "believe me, a time is coming when you will worship the Father neither on this mountain nor in Jerusalem. You Samaritans worship what you do not know; we worship what we do know, for salvation is from the Jews. Yet a time is coming and has now come when the true worshipers will worship the Father in the Spirit and in truth, for they are the kind of worshipers the Father seeks. God is spirit, and his worshipers must worship in the Spirit and in truth."

The woman said, "I know that Messiah" (called Christ) "is coming. When he comes, he will explain everything to us." Then Jesus declared, "I, the one speaking to you—I am he." Just then his disciples returned and were surprised to find him talking with a woman. But no one asked, "What do you want?" or "Why are you talking with her?" Then, leaving her water jar, the woman went back to the town and said to the people, "Come, see a man who told me everything I ever did. Could this be the Messiah?" They came out of the town and made their way toward him.

- John 4:5-30

Read John 4:5-30

Do you feel empty?

In speaking to the woman at the well, Jesus says, *"If only you knew* the gift God has for you and who you are speaking to. You would ask me, and I would give you living water."

If only you knew...

If only you knew the things God has in store for you...

If only you would take the time to know Him, and taste and see that He alone is good.

Like the woman at the well, maybe you feel completely empty. If you feel this way, you are most certainly not alone.

She almost missed what was right before her. She was talking to the One... Do you see it? The One... The One who could completely fill the emptiness and void inside of her....

She had completely misdiagnosed how to fill the tragic emptiness inside. Instead, she tightly clung to man after man after man. She tried to fill the void, but here she was...at the well...and still as thirsty as ever.

Unfortunately, people have feelings of spiritual emptiness from time to time, both believers and non-believers...Just like the woman at the well, there is a deep dark desolate place seemingly sucking the joy out of your life. An innate feeling lingers inside like the course you are eating is missing the main ingredient. And though you are consuming life, you leave the table still in want.

And you come to the wells of life expecting something satisfying, but there is only a temporary drink that leaves you in a worse state than before. In the end, you come to the well expecting something that quenches the thirst of emptiness, so you drink and drink and drink, but you are still left unsatisfied.

For this woman it was a person, but what is it for you?

What are you using to try and fill the emptiness inside?

Substances, people, activity, emotional outburst, food, appearance? It doesn't matter what we use, we will always end up feeling empty again.

> *Jesus is the only water that continually satisfies.*

Reflect:

Ask the Lord to reveal the areas of your life you have chosen to try to fill the emptiness…the affections to which you have given yourself which will simply never satisfy.

Write out or draw representations of everything the Holy Spirit reveals.

Engage:

You don't have to continue to feel empty. Grab an empty glass and prayerfully ask the Father to fill you in a supernaturally divine manner.

ONLY GOD CAN TRULY SATISFY! Emptiness cannot be filled by what we do, but only through His presence. Ask the Father to help you leave temporary satisfactions behind in exchange for His thirst-quenching divine presence. Fill the emptiness of the glass as you pour yourself a glass of cold water and drink it prayerfully asking the Father to help you see Him alone as your source of strength.

Notes:

DAY 10

"Knowing that I am not the one in control gives great encouragement. Knowing the One who is in control is everything"

- ALEXANDER MICHAEL

Now Naaman was commander of the army of the king of Aram. He was a great man in the sight of his master and highly regarded, because through him the Lord had given victory to Aram. He was a valiant soldier, but he had leprosy.

Now bands of raiders from Aram had gone out and had taken captive a young girl from Israel, and she served Naaman's wife. She said to her mistress, "If only my master would see the prophet who is in Samaria! He would cure him of his leprosy."

Naaman went to his master and told him what the girl from Israel had said. "By all means, go," the king of Aram replied. "I will send a letter to the king of Israel." So Naaman left, taking with him ten talents of silver, six thousand shekels of gold and ten sets of clothing. The letter that he took to the king of Israel read: "With this letter I am sending my servant Naaman to you so that you may cure him of his leprosy."

As soon as the king of Israel read the letter, he tore his robes and said, "Am I God? Can I kill and bring back to life? Why does this fellow send someone to me to be cured of his leprosy? See how he is trying to pick a quarrel with me!"

When Elisha the man of God heard that the king of Israel had torn his robes, he sent him this message: "Why have you torn your robes? Have the man come to me and he will know that there is a prophet in Israel." So

Naaman went with his horses and chariots and stopped at the door of Elisha's house. Elisha sent a messenger to say to him, "Go, wash yourself seven times in the Jordan, and your flesh will be restored and you will be cleansed."

But Naaman went away angry and said, "I thought that he would surely come out to me and stand and call on the name of the Lord his God, wave his hand over the spot and cure me of my leprosy. Are not Abana and Pharpar, the rivers of Damascus, better than all the waters of Israel? Couldn't I wash in them and be cleansed?" So he turned and went off in a rage.

Naaman's servants went to him and said, "My father, if the prophet had told you to do some great thing, would you not have done it? How much more, then, when he tells you, 'Wash and be cleansed'!" So he went down and dipped himself in the Jordan seven times, as the man of God had told him, and his flesh was restored and became clean like that of a young boy.

- 2 Kings 5:1-4

Read 2 Kings 5:1-14

Naaman was frantic for help, desperate for healing, but he almost squandered his healing because he wasn't willing to embrace the strange way God wanted to heal him. His diagnosis brought despair, but his doubt almost led to his absolute destruction. It did not make sense to Namaan. What was different about the waters here than in his own country? Surely God would utilize some grand miraculous event instead of merely dipping in the common waters of the land. This is not the way Namaan would choose to heal himself, surely God would do it another way.

Has this ever happened to you?
Have you ever found yourself in a position of doubt or anger because God wasn't doing things the way you wanted Him to?
Are you such a control freak that you order God around through "prayer"?

It is not about understanding the unattainable thoughts of God, it is about learning to trust Him wholly!

Namaan was accustomed to being in charge; he was familiar with possessing authority. The scriptures declare he was the "commander of the army of the king of Syria." Namaan gave orders and people followed his command. Though humbled by his illness, this sickened superior still rebelled against circumstances outside of his control and understanding.

It is entirely possible to be present in the right atmosphere and yet still unwilling to fully trust Him.

Perhaps he was insulted by the simplicity, perhaps he was unimpressed with the method, or more than likely the reality he was experiencing was far different than the expectations he had going on in his mind.

You cannot control God!

He is not a genie waiting to be beckoned in the world through the rubbing of a lamp in prayer. He is so much more.

"For my thoughts are not your thoughts, neither are your ways my ways, saith the LORD. For as the heavens are higher than the earth, so are my

ways higher than your ways, and my thoughts than your thoughts."
– Isaiah 55:8-9 KJV

> ***Attempting to control God is a glaring
> symptom of arrogance.***

Reflect:

In what ways are you being challenged to trust God amid circumstances
that do not make sense?

Have you attempted to control your own circumstances instead of
completely trusting in God?

Engage:

It's time to relinquish control. Clasp your hands as tight as you possibly
can. Imagine you are holding on to the things the Holy Spirit identified.
Ask the Father to help you to trust Him fully. As an act of surrender open
your hands up towards God and joyfully give up control.

Notes:

DAY 11

*"There are three stages in the work of God: Impossible;
Difficult; Done"*

- HUDSON TAYLOR

And Elijah said to Ahab, "Go, eat and drink, for there is the sound of a heavy rain." So Ahab went off to eat and drink, but Elijah climbed to the top of Carmel, bent down to the ground and put his face between his knees.

"Go and look toward the sea," he told his servant. And he went up and looked.
"There is nothing there," he said.
Seven times Elijah said, "Go back."

The seventh time the servant reported, "A cloud as small as a man's hand is rising from the sea."
So Elijah said, "Go and tell Ahab, 'Hitch up your chariot and go down before the rain stops you.'"

Meanwhile, the sky grew black with clouds, the wind rose, a heavy rain started falling and Ahab rode off to Jezreel.

- 1 Kings 18:41-45

Read 1 Kings 18:41-45

Have you ever had a hard season of life? Maybe you had a family member or a friend pass away? Did you get bullied at school or even at home? Maybe something big happened in your life recently and you did not know how to handle it or get past it? Has someone done something to you that has left unspeakable scars in your life you cannot seem to overcome? Do you have what seems like irreparable emotional or physical damage? Maybe you don't even want to move on?

Read verse 43 again. Notice how the servant says, "there is nothing there".

Have you ever had the thought that despite all your praying and asking there just seemed to be nothing there? A general sense of hopelessness? Despite your greatest efforts, you begin to believe there's no escape from the prison of this moment. What you were wanting was not there. "There is simply "nothing there".

You've asked God to do something…
You have asked God to intervene…
You have asked the Father to overcome…
You have asked for hope to reign…
You have asked for rain…
And the report keeps coming back "there is nothing there."

In the middle of this event notice, Elijah never abandons the reverent position of being on his knees. Why? Why remain on your knees despite the continual pronouncement that it was not raining? He knew what was going on physically was not an accurate representation. The absence of a cloud did not mean there wasn't rain, it just meant it wasn't there yet.

Elijah knew his eyes could provide a bleak outlook, but God had something else in store.

The physical realm was not indicative of what was going on in the spiritual realm. He could have left his place of prayer but there was something stirring in the heavenlies that had not manifested in the physical realm yet.

> *Difficulties are merely on-ramps to*
> *highways of heavenly intervention!*

Reflect:

Are you operating by what your eyes see or by what God is speaking? What voice are you listening to?

Identify the areas of your life where you have felt a sense of hopelessness and a lack of fruit.

Engage:

Close your eyes, hit your knees, and lift your concerns to the Lord. Ask him to help you develop a new perspective… a perspective far superseding what you perceive with your own eyes. When a new perspective has been received, get off your knees and expectantly wait and watch for a season of rain that conquers the drought.

Notes:

DAY 12

"I have learned to use the word 'impossible' with the greatest caution"

- WERNHER VON BRAUN

For though we live in the world, we do not wage war as the world does. The weapons we fight with are not the weapons of the world. On the contrary, they have divine power to demolish strongholds.

- 2 Corinthians 10:3-4

Read 2 Corinthians 10:3-4

What is a stronghold? This is the sole occurrence of the term in the New Testament, and it is of grave importance. A stronghold is a place that has been strategically developed to not be easily overcome. Like a fortified castle, there are many strongholds that appear to usurp power of our lives. Paul isn't saying that we as believers can tear down castles; he uses the terminology to depict circumstances and battles which will be difficult to surmount. But according to Paul, you and I have been given the power to overcome these strongholds.

What are the "strongholds" or "fortifications" with which we contend? In the very next verse, Paul interprets the metaphor: "We demolish arguments and every pretension that sets itself up against the knowledge of God, and we take captive every thought to make it obedient to Christ". The "pretension" is anything that sets itself up against God.

To Paul's audience, their most obvious strongholds were pride and arrogance.

What is it for you? What is your greatest inner struggle?

Read 2 Corinthians 10:4-5 again. YES, READ IT AGAIN!

> *Strongholds become sanctuaries when they encounter King Jesus.*

Places that seemed impenetrable can become beacons of heavenly breakthroughs. The Lord has given us His divine power to overcome these areas of our life. We can, through prayer and the power of the Holy Spirit, overcome.

Reflect:

Ask the Holy Spirit to identify the strongholds in your life.

Ask the Lord to defeat the stronghold that has overwhelmed you for far too long. Spend as much time with Him as you need.

Engage:

Grab a rock or another object you can crush with a hammer and use a marker to write or draw a description of the stronghold in your life. Ask the Father for His divine power to overcome the stronghold. As you sense the freedom, crush the rock with the hammer as a symbol of demolishing the stronghold in your life.

Notes:

DAY 13

"Waiting is God's school, wherein we learn some of His most valuable lessons"

- AUTHOR UNKNOWN

For though we live in the world, we do not wage war as the world does. The weapons we fight with are not the weapons of the world. On the contrary, they have divine power to demolish strongholds.

- Psalm 39:7

I wait for the Lord, my whole being waits,
and in his word I put my hope.
I wait for the Lord
more than watchmen wait for the morning,
more than watchmen wait for the morning.

- Psalm 130:5-6

The Lord is good to those whose hope is in him,
to the one who seeks him;

- Lamentations 3:25

but those who hope in the Lord
will renew their strength.
They will soar on wings like eagles;
they will run and not grow weary,
they will walk and not be faint.

- Isaiah 40:31

Read Psalm 39:7, Psalm 130:5-6, Lamentations 3:25, Isaiah 40:31

Nobody really likes to wait. I do not know anyone who has ever prayed to God and asked for the blessing of feverishly waiting on God to show their unconditional trust in Him. Waiting is not fun; in fact, it flat out stinks! While waiting is not easy, it is often necessary as a follower of Christ.

With the evolution of instantaneous access to unimaginable scores of knowledge, we have created Christ followers who make demands on God instead of learning to trust Him through the gloriously refining process of waiting. We prefer the microwave over the crockpot. We settle for dried-out radiated meat instead of waiting for the succulent juicy process of Holy Spirit truths.

For some reason, we have more problems waiting on spiritual matters than anything else. We will wait hours on end for the opening of a movie or a grand sale at our favorite department store, but we demand instantaneous answers from God. Oh, the irony!

Because of this difficulty, most of us will prematurely abandon the process of spiritual growth and, in so doing, we are in essence saying to the King "I don't trust you," "I can do better without you," and "You are not worth it."

In the middle of our struggle, there are continual admonitions from the Lord on the blessings and strength that accompanies those who wait.

Don't make the mistake of not waiting, because ...

> *The only thing harder than waiting on God*
> *- is wishing you would have.*

In waiting we express a confident expectation that God is working no matter how things speak to the contrary.

Reflect:

Where are you getting the opportunity to wait upon something special from the Lord?

How has waiting produced godly character in you which would not have been produced otherwise?

In what area can you express confident expectations that God is working on your behalf?

Engage:

Grab a pot, add water to it, and place it on the stove to begin the boiling process. You may even want to use this prayerful time to prepare a dish. There is an adage that a "watched pot never boils." Of course, the water eventually begins to boil, but as you watch, it seems never to begin boiling. Stand over the pot and wait for it to boil. Prayerfully and carefully stand near it but do not utter a word. Allow the Holy Spirit to reveal areas of your life where you have been impatient with the process of transformation. After the water begins to boil, turn it off, open your mouth before the Creator, and ask for the strength to continue the journey of faithfulness.

Notes:

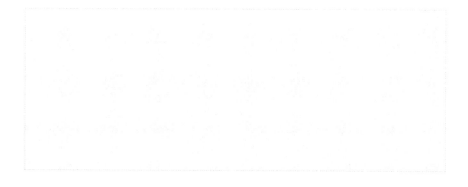

47

DAY 14

A prophecy: The word of the Lord to Israel through Malachi.
"I have loved you," says the Lord. "But you ask, 'How have you loved us?'

- Malachi 1:1-2

"A son honors his father, and a slave his master. If I am a father, where is the honor due me? If I am a master, where is the respect due me?" says the Lord Almighty.
"It is you priests who show contempt for my name.
"But you ask, 'How have we shown contempt for your name?'

"By offering defiled food on my altar.
"But you ask, 'How have we defiled you?'
"By saying that the Lord's table is contemptible. [8] When you offer blind animals for sacrifice, is that not wrong? When you sacrifice lame or diseased animals, is that not wrong? Try offering them to your governor! Would he be pleased with you? Would he accept you?" says the Lord Almighty.

"Now plead with God to be gracious to us. With such offerings from your hands, will he accept you?"—says the Lord Almighty.

"Oh, that one of you would shut the temple doors, so that you would not light useless fires on my altar! I am not pleased with you," says the Lord Almighty, "and I will accept no offering from your hands. [11] My name will be great among the nations, from where the sun rises to where it sets. In every place incense and pure offerings will be brought to me, because my name will be great among the nations," says the Lord Almighty.

"But you profane it by saying, 'The Lord's table is defiled,' and, 'Its food is contemptible.'

- Malachi 1:6-12

Read Malachi 1:1-2, 6-12

Here is a group who has literally been sustained by the very hands of God, yet they arrogantly respond by saying, "How have you loved us?" Oh, how easy it is to forget! The Israelites had seen the mighty hand of the incomparable God come to their aid time and time again. There should have been no doubt of the Father's love for His people, yet they selfishly question the undeniable love of the Creator towards His creation. They had grown cold to the divine interactions that had been lavishly poured out on them.

How quick we are to grow accustomed to the supernatural grace freely given to us! How freely we dismiss the obvious acts of kindness given to us by our Designer! If we are not careful, our familiarity with the things of God can produce contempt within the walls of our very own heart just like the Israelites.

When God surveyed the whole of human history, he did not spare any expense, He offered his best for us, and we should be inclined to do so for him as well.

As a result of growing cold to God, the Israelites began offering something less than their absolute best. Instead of offering the finest of their flock in sacrifice, they brought crippled, polluted offerings before the Lord.

The Lord's response is not only gut-wrenching and dreadful; it is very convicting even for us as believers today. Within the heights of the elaborate lives we have built for ourselves emerges the glaring deficiency of our dedication to God. We give all our energy, time, and finances to worldly desires, but when it comes to the Divine, we bring our leftovers. Or worse, we willfully choose to gratify our own desires over the kingdom.

> *You don't bring a sick goat to a great king.*

Reflect:

Why does God desire our best?

In what ways are you offering something that is less than your best to God?

How can you willfully choose to put God first in your life?

Engage:

Refuse to eat anything fresh today. Only eat leftovers! If none are available, willingly choose to eat things you do not like. Each time ask the Lord to remind you to give Him your best continually.

Notes:

DAY 15

"The best way to have your faith strengthened is to have communion with Christ"

- C.H. SPURGEON

There he went into a cave and spent the night. And the word of the Lord came to him: "What are you doing here, Elijah?"

He replied, "I have been very zealous for the Lord God Almighty. The Israelites have rejected your covenant, torn down your altars, and put your prophets to death with the sword. I am the only one left, and now they are trying to kill me too."

The Lord said, "Go out and stand on the mountain in the presence of the Lord, for the Lord is about to pass by."

Then a great and powerful wind tore the mountains apart and shattered the rocks before the Lord, but the Lord was not in the wind. After the wind there was an earthquake, but the Lord was not in the earthquake. After the earthquake came a fire, but the Lord was not in the fire. And after the fire came a gentle whisper. When Elijah heard it, he pulled his cloak over his face and went out and stood at the mouth of the cave.

Then a voice said to him, "What are you doing here, Elijah?"

He replied, "I have been very zealous for the Lord God Almighty. The Israelites have rejected your covenant, torn down your altars, and put your prophets to death with the sword. I am the only one left, and now they are trying to kill me too."

The Lord said to him, "Go back the way you came, and go to the Desert of Damascus. When you get there, anoint Hazael king over Aram. [16] Also, anoint Jehu son of Nimshi king over Israel, and anoint Elisha son of Shaphat from Abel Meholah to succeed you as prophet. Jehu will put to death any who escape the sword of Hazael, and Elisha will put to death any who escape the sword of Jehu. Yet I reserve seven thousand in Israel— all whose knees have not bowed down to Baal and whose mouths have not kissed him."

- 1 Kings 19:9-18

Read 1 Kings 19:9-18

"What are you doing here Elijah?" Wow, what a question. Elijah has seen God perform miracles right in front of his eyes, but in this unfortunate moment of weakness he runs away and begins to pout. After clamoring to God about his isolation, the compassionate rebuke of the Lord utters six of the most terrifying words in all of scripture, "What are you doing here Elijah?"

I cannot conceive a more alarming question than for the King over all creation to utter the words, "What are you doing here?" What a startling and convicting statement! I cannot imagine what all quaked within the body of Elijah at that moment, but I can easily fathom the depths of confusion, chaos, and failure that had to be running through his head.

God had just defeated the prophets of Baal and literal fire rained down from heaven. At the news of the defeat, Jezebel, the wicked Queen, issues a death threat to Elijah. Instead of invoking the power and might of the God who just defeated over 400 prophets of a false god, Elijah chooses to run from a single wicked female. God can handle over 400 prophets and water-soaked wood, but He cannot handle an evil woman? These volatile thoughts invaded Elijah's mind as he stood facing that glaring question, "What are you doing here?"

In a sense God could ask many of us that same question, "What are you doing here (insert name)?"

> *Godly confidence is the child of trust birthed by holy union with the Almighty*

53

Reflect:

Reflect on a time when you found yourself in a position you should not be in as a son or daughter of God.

Where and when have you found yourself in a position doubting the power and protection of your King?

Is there anything in your life to which the same words could be issued to you as a follower of Christ right now?

What position, state, or circumstance are you currently experiencing because of not trusting in the Almighty?

Engage:

If weather permits, go outside or to a local park and sit under a tree like Elijah. Reread the passage again and let the Father speak. Ask the King to reveal any areas of self-pity or disobedience. As He does, list them out in the Notes section. Do not merely stop with this revelation! Allow the compassionate whisper of the Lord to fill your soul. Close by whispering your own prayer as a response.

Notes:

DAY 16

"and let us not grow weary in well doing: for in due season we shall reap, if we faint not"

- GALATIANS 6:9

Now Ahab told Jezebel everything Elijah had done and how he had killed all the prophets with the sword. So Jezebel sent a messenger to Elijah to say, "May the gods deal with me, be it ever so severely, if by this time tomorrow I do not make your life like that of one of them."

Elijah was afraid and ran for his life. When he came to Beersheba in Judah, he left his servant there, while he himself went a day's journey into the wilderness. He came to a broom bush, sat down under it and prayed that he might die. "I have had enough, Lord," he said. "Take my life; I am no better than my ancestors." Then he lay down under the bush and fell asleep.

All at once an angel touched him and said, "Get up and eat." He looked around, and there by his head was some bread baked over hot coals, and a jar of water. He ate and drank and then lay down again.

The angel of the Lord came back a second time and touched him and said, "Get up and eat, for the journey is too much for you." So he got up and ate and drank. Strengthened by that food, he traveled forty days and forty nights until he reached Horeb, the mountain of God. There he went into a cave and spent the night.

And the word of the Lord came to him: "What are you doing here, Elijah?"

He replied, "I have been very zealous for the Lord God Almighty. The Israelites have rejected your covenant, torn down your altars, and put your prophets to death with the sword. I am the only one left, and now they are trying to kill me too."

The Lord said, "Go out and stand on the mountain in the presence of the Lord, for the Lord is about to pass by."

Then a great and powerful wind tore the mountains apart and shattered the rocks before the Lord, but the Lord was not in the wind. After the wind there was an earthquake, but the Lord was not in the earthquake. After the earthquake came a fire, but the Lord was not in the fire. And after the fire came a gentle whisper. When Elijah heard it, he pulled his cloak over his face and went out and stood at the mouth of the cave.

Then a voice said to him, "What are you doing here, Elijah?"

He replied, "I have been very zealous for the Lord God Almighty. The Israelites have rejected your covenant, torn down your altars, and put your prophets to death with the sword. I am the only one left, and now they are trying to kill me too."

The Lord said to him, "Go back the way you came, and go to the Desert of Damascus. When you get there, anoint Hazael king over Aram. Also, anoint Jehu son of Nimshi king over Israel, and anoint Elisha son of Shaphat from Abel Meholah to succeed you as prophet. Jehu will put to death any who escape the sword of Hazael, and Elisha will put to death any who escape the sword of Jehu. Yet I reserve seven thousand in Israel— all whose knees have not bowed down to Baal and whose mouths have not kissed him."

- 1 Kings 19:1-18

Read 1 Kings 19:1-18

Elijah precludes his mountaintop victory over the prophets of Baal by retreating to a hill where he feverishly cries out to God for his life to be taken. Within the Lord's response is a truth that rattles the foundations of many of us. Elijah pleads his case with the Lord but eventually, the loving Father responds with words that undoubtedly shook the prophet to his core, "Get up…go" (v. 15). It wasn't that God was unconcerned with Elijah's state of mind or somehow dismissing his dreadful feeling, the Father knew there was still more to do.

The battle wasn't over; the race had not yet been finished. God wasn't done with Elijah yet, and He is not finished with you either! Hear the words of the Eternal Father softly yet powerfully speaking the same words to you, "Get up…go."

Have you ever felt like you were finished, like the book to your spiritual or physical journey had already been completed? Whether from failure or false pride, you felt like you crossed the tape of the finish line and have completed the race?

The evidence you have not finished is magnified by the undeniable fact the Maker has still allowed you to be present in this creation.

> *The concluding chapter of your life has not yet been written, so, finish well.*

While you are still breathing, choose to serve the King with all your might and all your strength!

Reflect:

What tasks have you abandoned that need to be finished?

What can you do with the time you have been given to bring glory to the King?

What can God do with a fully devoted version of yourself?

Engage:

Following the stark rebuke of Elijah are some of the most comforting words, "Get up…go". Elijah had to physically move from one position to another. He moved from "Here" to "There". Designate two areas you can walk in between. Label one as "Here" and the other as "There". Start at the area marked here. While standing in location one take time to confess the expanses of your life where you have allowed fear and a lack of trust to reign. Prayerfully move from location one to your second position. As you do ask the Lord where you need to "get up and go". Thank God for His nearness and commit to moving forward in your relationship with Him.

Notes:

DAY 17

*"When I fancied that I stood alone I was really in the
ridiculous position of being backed up by all of Christendom"*

- G.K. CHESTERTON

There he went into a cave and spent the night.

And the word of the Lord came to him: "What are you doing here, Elijah?"

He replied, "I have been very zealous for the Lord God Almighty. The Israelites have rejected your covenant, torn down your altars, and put your prophets to death with the sword. I am the only one left, and now they are trying to kill me too."

The Lord said, "Go out and stand on the mountain in the presence of the Lord, for the Lord is about to pass by."

Then a great and powerful wind tore the mountains apart and shattered the rocks before the Lord, but the Lord was not in the wind. After the wind there was an earthquake, but the Lord was not in the earthquake. After the earthquake came a fire, but the Lord was not in the fire. And after the fire came a gentle whisper. When Elijah heard it, he pulled his cloak over his face and went out and stood at the mouth of the cave.

Then a voice said to him, "What are you doing here, Elijah?"

He replied, "I have been very zealous for the Lord God Almighty. The Israelites have rejected your covenant, torn down your altars, and put your prophets to death with the sword. I am the only one left, and now they are trying to kill me too."

The Lord said to him, "Go back the way you came, and go to the Desert of Damascus. When you get there, anoint Hazael king over Aram. Also, anoint Jehu son of Nimshi king over Israel, and anoint Elisha son of Shaphat from Abel Meholah to succeed you as prophet. Jehu will put to death any who escape the sword of Hazael, and Elisha will put to death any who escape the sword of Jehu. Yet I reserve seven thousand in Israel—all whose knees have not bowed down to Baal and whose mouths have not kissed him."

- 1 Kings 19:9-18

Read 1 Kings 19-9-18

I'm sure if you would have asked Elijah early on his ministry if he ever would have asked the Lord to take his life, he would have adamantly resounded, "There is absolutely no way." If you would have asked the prophet if he would have found himself griping to God about being alone, he would have said, "I just need the Father." Isolation, however, has a way of coloring your perspective with a deep dark tone you did not even know existed, the darkness of which you thought would never color the foundations of your own life. There is a reason isolation is considered a punishment in prison.

Isolation is sometimes willful and deliberate while at other times the byproduct of our circumstances; yet its results are almost always deadly. Isolation is something mankind has struggled with from the beginning. In Gen 2:8 the Creator comments, "it's not good for man to be alone." Even the noted thinker Albert Einstein once commented, "It is strange to be known so universally, and yet to be so lonely". God did not intend for us to be alone. Isolation is a breeding ground for the enemy's lies.

In a world of numerous social media communities, we deceptively appear more connected than ever. This masked reality has led to a dreadful state of loneliness in scores of people. We gage our value based upon the momentary click of a stranger mindlessly scrolling through newsfeeds. This so-called community is determined not by genuine authentic relationships but rather by the outlying number of likes we get on any particular post during the day. We have more ways than ever to remain connected, but they generally are false representations of true community.

It is impossible to be in community while constructing walls of isolation.

Reflect:

How can you connect with others for the good of the kingdom?

What relationships has the Lord given you to encourage you to know Him more?

Who has God placed in your life to encourage, strengthen, and support?

What can you do to be a vital part of the community where God has placed you?

Engage:

Pick up the phone and call someone the Lord has resolutely and divinely placed in your life. If you feel like you do not have anyone, ask the Holy Spirit to reveal someone He has purposefully positioned around you. After reaching out to him or her, be intentional. Pray together and encourage one another in the Lord.

Notes:

DAY 18

"God has cast our confessed sins into the depths of the sea,
and He's even put a "No fishing" sign over the spot"

\- D.L. MOODY

Who is a God like you,
who pardons sin and forgives the transgression
of the remnant of his inheritance?
You do not stay angry forever
but delight to show mercy.

You will again have compassion on us;
you will tread our sins underfoot
and hurl all our iniquities into the depths of the sea.

\- Micah 7:18-19

"I, even I, am he who blots out
your transgressions, for my own sake,
and remembers your sins no more.

\- Isaiah 43:25

Read Micah 7:18-19, Isaiah 43:25

In both passages God reminds Israel of His faithfulness though Israel had a long, epic history of deliberately and willfully abandoning God for sinful and lude acts. Despite all this, the Father still promised a future day when He would "hurl all their sins into the depths of the sea". Thankfully, the promised Messiah, Jesus, transformed this hope into our current reality.

Within the book of Micah, the Messiah is seen as the One freeing us from the consequences of our transgressions. In the book of Isaiah, He promises to actually forget our sins! Can you imagine that?! The God who created all things, sustains all things, and knows all things, makes a conscious decision to FORGET our transgressions against Him...

Yet if we were all honest, many of us continue to hold on to things in our past because we simply cannot forgive ourselves. We cannot seem to let go. There is a strange familiarity bearing the weight of regret. Despite our desire to be forgiven, we often bear the weight of our sin though freedom is readily available. But why?

We live as if God has a footnote at the bottom of the passage in Micah that reads, "God promises to hurl all your sins into the depths of the ocean, BUT if you committed [insert your horrible sin] then, well, He's going to hold it against you".

That is a lie straight from the pits of hell!

Hear the words of God as they penetrate the darkness...

"If we confess our sins, He is faithful and just to forgive us our sins and purify us from all unrighteousness" – 1 John 1:9

Reflect:

Sit before the King and allow the Holy Spirit to reveal any sin in your life. Do not rush in and out of this moment. Allow the kindness of God to reveal areas of your life where you have been blinded, become numb, or blatantly engaged in sin.

Engage:

Spend some time in prayer confessing any sin you may have while you ask the Merciful King to forgive you. Grab a note card or piece of paper and list out the sins that you have allowed to haunt you forever. Shame, guilt, and despair are not characteristics of someone walking in the Spirit. Allow the lord's forgiveness to wash over you.

Take the paper and prayerfully go outside to a place that is quiet.

God has already done His task. He has chosen to not only forgive you, but to hurl those sins into the depths of the ocean! You have the opportunity right now to allow that forgiveness to work in your life, but only if you are willing to accept it and not hold onto things from your past. Dig a small hole and bury the note card / paper as a symbol of taking on the mind of Christ and not allowing the guilt and shame of the enemy to reign over you. Bury it and never let it come to your mind again. Walk in the Freedom the Lord has graciously bestowed upon you.

Notes:

DAY 19

"Perseverance in prayer is the annihilation of sloth"

- JOHN CLIMACUS

Do not merely listen to the word, and so deceive yourselves. Do what it says.

- James 1:22

Whatever you do, work at it with all your heart, as working for the Lord, not for human masters,

- Colossians 3:23

Then the man who had received one bag of gold came. 'Master,' he said, 'I knew that you are a hard man, harvesting where you have not sown and gathering where you have not scattered seed. So I was afraid and went out and hid your gold in the ground. See, here is what belongs to you.' "His master replied, 'You wicked, lazy servant! So you knew that I harvest where I have not sown and gather where I have not scattered seed? Well then, you should have put my money on deposit with the bankers, so that when I returned I would have received it back with interest. "So take the bag of gold from him and give it to the one who has ten bags. For whoever has will be given more, and they will have an abundance. Whoever does not have, even what they have will be taken from them. And throw that worthless servant outside, into the darkness, where there will be weeping and gnashing of teeth.'

- Matthew 25:24-30

Do your best to present yourself to God as one approved, a worker who does not need to be ashamed and who correctly handles the word of truth.

- 2 Timothy 2:15

Read James 1:22, Colossians 3:23, Matthew 25:24-30, 2 Timothy 2:15

It is often said that we envy the grass being greener on the other side, but the truth is most of us are not willing to intentionally labor towards the desired result we've coveted from across the fence.

There isn't a one of us who hasn't struggled with laziness at one point or another. Maybe you feel sluggish to get out of bed and pray in the morning, maybe you've grown weary of simple spiritual disciplines, maybe you've grown complacent towards sharing the gospel, or your ear has grown callous to the Holy Spirit. Slowly and assuredly laziness has crept in, and with it a callous and unresponsive heart.

> ### *This is the laziest generation of Christ followers to bear the name Christian.*

We have more commentaries, more expositions, and more access to knowledge concerning the scriptures than ever before, but for some reason, we are the least moved to action. We are quick to make promises, but very few of us make commitments.

> ### *Biblically academic, spiritually anemic.*

Too often we are like the disciples in the garden of Gethsemane, a willing spirit, but weak in the flesh.

How do you know if your life is marked by spiritual laziness? One could completely disregard the simplest spiritual disciplines. More than not, spiritual laziness is often identified not by sitting around but rather most evidenced by busyness. We busy ourselves with temporal things instead of eternal things. Our perspective shifts from the kingdom to the things of this world.

Spiritual growth is not the product of occasional supernatural events but rather the ongoing and continual application of the simplest matters of spiritual discipline. Prayer, studying, and fasting are not items for the mature to leave behind as they move towards their goal, but rather the primary gateways for maturity in the kingdom.

Reflect:

What has dominated your thoughts more than the Gospel?

What areas of discipline have you been prone to allow laziness to creep in?

How has spiritual laziness negatively impacted your relationship with the King?

Engage:

Write out a plan to overcome the spiritual laziness that has crept into your life. Challenge yourself not with occasional events but consistently applying the spiritual principles you know we have been given to overcome. Set a disciplined schedule to help purposefully live out the purpose that Father has for you.

Notes:

DAY 20

"If I find in myself desires which nothing in this world can satisfy, the only logical explanation is that I was made for another world"

- C.S. LEWIS, MERE CHRISTIANITY

One of those days Jesus went out to a mountainside to pray, and spent the night praying to God. When morning came, he called his disciples to him and chose twelve of them, whom he also designated apostles: Simon (whom he named Peter), his brother Andrew, James, John, Philip, Bartholomew, Matthew, Thomas, James son of Alphaeus, Simon who was called the Zealot, Judas son of James, and Judas Iscariot, who became a traitor.

- Luke 6:12-16

Read Luke 6:12-16

Christianity has universally labeled Judas a traitor, but he was unequivocally so much more. Judas was first known as an apostle and was numbered among those steadfastly following Jesus. He heard the teachings of Jesus first-hand; he witnessed the miracles of Jesus with his very own eyes, but something happened in Him that if we are not careful can also happen within us.

> *You can be in the right places, with the right people, and still completely miss it!*

Judas left his family to follow Christ, he was on mission, he told people about the Messiah…so what happened? How could he be that close to Jesus and miss who He truly was?

Read Matthew 26:14

"What are you willing to give me if I deliver him to you?" Judas was willing to exchange Jesus for something else. Judas's sin wasn't merely greed, it was that he was willing to take anything at all in exchange for Jesus. Judas traded intimacy with Jesus for a mere thirty coins. Some would argue the sum of the money was not enough but there is simply no amount grand enough to compete. If all the power and money in the world would have been offered, it still would have failed in comparison to Jesus! There is no negotiation comparable to the value of walking with Christ.

Reflect:

Many of us are just like Judas. You say, "I would never do that." What have you exchanged in place of intimacy with the King?

What or who have you willfully chosen over Jesus?

Where have you sold yourself into sin instead of denying yourself?

What sin have you willfully chosen to be temporarily satisfied in instead of walking wholly in His presence?

What are your thirty pieces of silver?

Engage:

There is absolutely nothing worth the exchange! Put excessive amounts of coins in your pocket and let it rattle around all day long. Every time you feel it, be reminded of the tendency of your exchange, and choose intimacy and holiness instead. Every time you are reminded, stop, and ask the Father to awaken you to His enduring presence.

Notes:

DAY 21

"The reason why men do not look to the Church today is that she has destroyed her own influence by compromise"

- G. CAMPBELL MORGAN

The Reubenites and Gadites, who had very large herds and flocks, saw that the lands of Jazer and Gilead were suitable for livestock. So they came to Moses and Eleazar the priest and to the leaders of the community, and said, "Ataroth, Dibon, Jazer, Nimrah, Heshbon, Elealeh, Sebam, Nebo and Beon— the land the Lord subdued before the people of Israel—are suitable for livestock, and your servants have livestock. If we have found favor in your eyes," they said, "let this land be given to your servants as our possession. Do not make us cross the Jordan."

- Numbers 32:1-5

Read Numbers 32:1-5

This is perhaps one of the saddest stories in all the scriptures, and it is often looked over, dismissed, or even written off as the sovereign plan of God. There is so much more here than what meets the eye.

The land east of the Jordan had everything it needed to be plentiful. When the two and a half tribes looked around, they saw everything pleasing to the eye and bountiful for raising crops. At their request, they are granted permission to stay east of the Jordan instead of crossing over. They made a reasonable choice based upon the physical conditions, but places of obedience are often not the most reasonable choices!

Partial obedience is still disobedience!

While it may appear like mere geography, it is so much more. The choice to stay east of the Jordan was a decision not to inherit the promised blessings of God. There they stood as close in proximity as was possible and they choose not to move west. They settled for something that looked good instead of something that was right! They chose a place of compromise over a place of obedience. So many believers today reek of compromise.

We act like God is some sort of accessory to be added to our outfit. Believers settle for a watered-down version of Christianity that is good enough to save us, but not great enough to exchange our entire lives for. That is not Christianity at all. Christianity is not merely an addition to one's life; it is the entirety of one's life. Do not settle! Do not let mediocrity and compromise reign in you as a child of the King.

East is not where you belong. Go west! No matter the difficulty of fording the river, head west.

Reflect:

What positions of compromise do we often choose over heading west?

What can you do to consciously begin to ford the river to a place of obedience west of the Jordan?

Engage:

Take a prayer walk today. Ask the Father to help you not choose a position of compromise in your life. As you pray, walk in a westerly direction as a symbol of choosing obedience over convenience and compromise.

Notes:

DAY 22

*"We are all pencils in the hand of a writing God, who is
sending love letters to the world"*

- MOTHER TERESA

Then the mother of Zebedee's sons came to Jesus with her sons and, kneeling down, asked a favor of him. "What is it you want?" he asked. She said, "Grant that one of these two sons of mine may sit at your right and the other at your left in your kingdom."

"You don't know what you are asking," Jesus said to them. "Can you drink the cup I am going to drink?" "We can," they answered. Jesus said to them, "You will indeed drink from my cup, but to sit at my right or left is not for me to grant. These places belong to those for whom they have been prepared by my Father."

When the ten heard about this, they were indignant with the two brothers. Jesus called them together and said, "You know that the rulers of the Gentiles lord it over them, and their high officials exercise authority over them. Not so with you. Instead, whoever wants to become great among you must be your servant, and whoever wants to be first must be your slave—just as the Son of Man did not come to be served, but to serve, and to give his life as a ransom for many."

- Matthew 20:20-28

When he had finished washing their feet, he put on his clothes and returned to his place. "Do you understand what I have done for you?" he asked them. "You call me 'Teacher' and 'Lord,' and rightly so, for that is what I am. Now that I, your Lord and Teacher, have washed your feet, you also should wash one another's feet. I have set you an example that you should do as I have done for you.

- John 13:12-15

He must become greater; I must become less."

- John 3:30

Read Matthew 20:20-28, John 13:12-15, John 3:30

We are naturally selfish people. Place a photo of a group in front of us and we instantly try to find ourselves before admiring anything else about the photography. In fact, our assessment of the photo is usually based solely on how we look in it, not others. When Jesus gives the stark challenge recorded in verse 28, the natural side of us doesn't necessarily leap for joy. In fact, when we genuinely serve others, it demands the humbling of oneself.

Luckily, Jesus didn't just talk about serving; He modeled it for us. In John 13 we read the beautiful account of Jesus washing the feet of those serving with Him. Jesus, the leader among his followers, stooped to the position of a servant and humbly washed the disciples' feet. In so doing, he provided a lasting example what we are to look like.

> *Serving others gives us admission into the movie of their life's transformation.*

Reflect:

Where is Christ calling you to serve?

Where can you selflessly give of yourself, not to be honored, but purely in order that the kingdom of God would increase?

What part of oneself do you need to die to in order to better serve others?

Engage:

Write the word "others" on your hand. As you see your hand throughout the day, ask yourself the question, "Am I serving others or am I serving myself?" Genuinely ask the Father to help you have heavenly vision as you interact and engage in the world around you. Be intentional and listen to the Holy Spirit as you make yourself available.

Notes:

DAY 23

"Bitterness is like cancer. It eats upon the host"

- AUTHOR UNKNOWN

Bear with each other and forgive one another if any of you has a grievance against someone. Forgive as the Lord forgave you.

- Colossians 3:13

Cast all your anxiety on him because he cares for you.

- 1 Peter 5:7

But he was pierced for our transgressions,
he was crushed for our iniquities;
the punishment that brought us peace was on him,
and by his wounds we are healed.

- Isaiah 53:5

He heals the brokenhearted
and binds up their wounds.

- Psalm 147:3

Read Colossians 3:13, 1 Peter 5:7, Isaiah 53:5, Psalm 147:3

You simply cannot be alive without experiencing wounds on your heart. It's impossible to exist without being hurt by someone at some point. It is inevitable; it is going to happen! Whether by other people, circumstances, or even your own decisions, all of us will experience pain and hurt at various points in our lives.

As Christians, the cross has provided everything we need to bring healing to every hurt we experience. The scriptures are bursting with encouragement from the cross.

With the cross there is HEALING,
there is LOVE,
there is PURPOSE,
there is FORGIVENESS,
there is ACCEPTANCE.
With the cross, there is EVERYTHING we need.

While many of us recognize the availability of the Father's divine intervention,

many of us willfully choose to "pick our scabs".

For some reason, we will not let things heal. We want others to know of our pain, recognize our loss, grasp how severe our wounds are so we "pick our scabs". We do not want to be hurt again so we tightly grip the scars not letting the Father completely step in.

Reflect:

Would you be willing to let go today? To really let go…not merely fake it, but to genuinely allow the Sovereign Healer to intervene and masterfully create a place of healing within the impenetrable walls of your calloused heart? His acceptance, His love, His healing is certainly available. Let the discomfort of your heart collide with the grace of the cross! Concede your will and your offense to the joy-filled forgiveness you, yourself, can experience.

Spend some time in prayer asking the Father to expose every region of your life where pain, hurt, and unforgiveness have reigned. Maybe you are someone with lots of small wounds, maybe you have massive wounds created by others. Your pain may have emanated from a person, a sin, words, a family member, or even more. Regardless of its origin, the cross provides an answer to all our hurts.

Engage:

Grab a couple of bandages from your house. Write every hurt/concern/pain on the bandage that comes to your mind. Reread the scriptures at the top of the page…

Spend some more time in prayer, embrace the silence as you allow the Father's presence to bring healing to your hurt. Take as long as you need. Don't move on until every scar is brought before King Jesus. If you are willing, take the bandage and stick it in your bible as a reminder of His healing.

Notes:

DAY 24

"Ephesians 5:18 is not just an experience to be enjoyed but a command to be obeyed. If we do not open ourselves to a daily encounter with the Holy Spirit, then the inevitable conclusion is that we are disobedient Christians"

- DWIGHT L. MOODY

For this reason I kneel before the Father, from whom every family in heaven and on earth derives its name. I pray that out of his glorious riches he may strengthen you with power through his Spirit in your inner being, so that Christ may dwell in your hearts through faith. And I pray that you, being rooted and established in love, may have power, together with all the Lord's holy people, to grasp how wide and long and high and deep is the love of Christ, and to know this love that surpasses knowledge—that you may be filled to the measure of all the fullness of God.

- Ephesians 3:14-19

Read Ephesians 3:14-19

The word "filled" in this verse is written in the grammatical tense which means "to continue to be filled over and over again." Many believers view their walk with Christ as a series of singular occurrences which rarely and occasionally occur instead of a frequent and persistent journey with the very real and present King. There are undeniably monumental moments where the King radically interrupts your life. Rejoice, these occurrences fuel you for the consistent, lifelong journey of walking with the Lord.

Paul deliberately uses this tense to awaken the believer to the mind-blowing understanding they can and should regularly be filled with the Spirit.

Why do we need to be filled continually? Just like our bodies, our soul becomes parched and weary when they are not filled.

> *The rumble of an empty stomach however cannot compare to the groaning of a soul that has not communed with God.*

Reflect:

Have you ever felt like you were running on empty? Have you ever found your soul desperately gasping for something that only His presence can provide? Some of us have been running on fumes for so long we have forgotten what it is like to be full.

All of this can change…today. It is not the sum of the mere knowledge of the holy scriptures coupled with persistent motivation, but rather as one who has the "strength to comprehend…the breadth and length and height and depth of the love of Christ."

What has led you to the place where you are so empty?

Engage:

Grab an empty glass from your cabinet. Stop and spend genuine time in the presence of the Father. Confess that you often feel like the glass before you, full of potential but completely empty. Ask the Lord to do what only He can do, to fill you to "the measure of fullness". Let your soul be filled – you may want to sit quietly, sing songs of praise, or continue to read His word. As a symbol of being filled, pour yourself a glass of cold refreshment and drink the entire contents.

Notes:

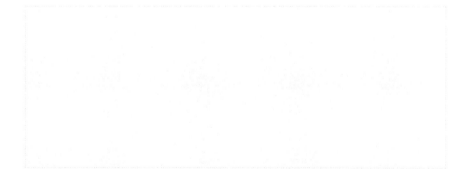

DAY 25

"The dearest idol I have known,
Whate'er that idol be,
Help me to tear it from thy throne,
And worship only Thee"

\- WILLIAM COOPER

Dear children, keep yourselves from idols.

\- 1 John 5:21

Read 1 John 5:21

At first glance, this appears to be one of the most random verses in the entire Bible. It is the last sentence of this letter, and it appears not to correspond with the immediate context of John's writing at all. As you reflect upon the text, however, you see exactly why he abruptly ended his letter in this manner. Deep inside the factory of John's mind, there was a message working that was so important it had to be shared with his readers no matter what. It was as if John was saying, "If you don't hear anything else, hear this...KEEP YOURSELVES FROM IDOLS."

What exactly was John referencing and why was it so vital that he included it as his closing remark? Surely those that claimed to be Christians would not be placing golden calves, wooden gods, or other idols all over their house. There had to be something else. These were believers he was addressing, not pagans. Why was it so important? John was overtly declaring, "If there is anything in your life taking priority over God – get rid of it!"

Idols are anything that take priority and value over God. Yes, anything!

In most cultures, idolatry abounds. Idols can take many forms, and though they may not be as overt as a golden calf, they are still prevalent in most peoples' lives. Whether it be our very own kids, food, or wealth, we all struggle with idols. It may be as subtle as a sporting event or as lambasting as pride.

We all masquerade as architects of idolatry

Why are idols so wrong? Because the King is so much better than anything this world has to offer. This does not mean you cannot enjoy creation; it means that creation cannot take priority over the Creator.

Everything fails in comparison to Christ.... everything! Or as the Psalmist put it, "Better is one day in your courts than a thousand days elsewhere." There is absolutely, positively nothing that even comes close in comparison to God.

Reflect:

Think carefully.

Would you be willing to let go of anything blockading your way from knowing Christ more?

Would you be willing to crush anything robbing you of your time with the Lord?

Would you willingly abandon that which has taken priority in your life over God?

Would you take sincere desperate measures to not only rid yourselves of but also crush the idols that are in your life?

It takes a radical commitment and radical adjustments to begin to eliminate things that have taken so much of our time and affection.

Engage:

Identify the idols in your life by listing them out on a sheet of paper. Ask the Father to allow you the beauty of seeing Him as so much better. When you have received your new perspective, throw the paper away or burn it as a symbol of destroying the value you allowed it to have in your life over the King.

When you are finished, thank God for being better, for being more, for being so much worthier of your time and energy.

Notes:

DAY 26

"Until men weep for sinners; sinners will not weep for their sins"

- L.R. SCARBOROUGH

Rend your heart
and not your garments.
Return to the Lord your God,
for he is gracious and compassionate,
slow to anger and abounding in love,
and he relents from sending calamity.

Who knows? He may turn and relent
and leave behind a blessing—
grain offerings and drink offerings
for the Lord your God.

Blow the trumpet in Zion,
declare a holy fast,
call a sacred assembly.

Gather the people,
consecrate the assembly;
bring together the elders,
gather the children,
those nursing at the breast.
Let the bridegroom leave his room
and the bride her chamber.

Let the priests, who minister before the Lord,
weep between the portico and the altar.
Let them say, "Spare your people, Lord.
Do not make your inheritance an object of scorn,
a byword among the nations.
Why should they say among the peoples,
'Where is their God?'"

- Joel 2:12-17

If my people, who are called by my name, will humble themselves and pray and seek my face and turn from their wicked ways, then I will hear from heaven, and I will forgive their sin and will heal their land.

- 2 Chronicles 7:14

Read Joel 2:12-17

When spiritual awakening appears, it will come as God's people begin to intercede, cry out, and become desperate for Him to move in the lives of people around them. Not because we have another retreat, another great message, or new exciting and passionate worship songs, but because a holy intervention beckoned the gracious ear of King Jesus.

Read 2 Chronicles 7:14

We have the distinct privilege of approaching Someone who has the power to radically change the atmosphere. Many critically charge the modern church with various accusations, believing they can attribute the lack of fruitfulness to poor programming or personalities while prayerlessness reigns in the halls of our worship centers and homes.

Who is feverishly and fervently approaching the throne room on the behalf of the adulterous bride? Who is asking the Father to move in their family's life? Their friend's life? Their church body? Their pastor's life?

> *The greatest sin of our culture isn't rooted in our bad theology, it is the poison of our prayerlessness.*

Read Joel 2:17 Again

The porch was located at the entrance of the temple and the altar was located at the other end of the building. So "between the porch and the altar" means their prayers were to fill the entire place. The priestly lament permeated the entire house of worship. The burden to pray did not flow from obligation, but from desperation.

Reflect:

Take some time to do the same...

How long has it been since you were so desperate to see God move that tears began to flow down your face? How long has it been since you were so burdened over someone's situation that you were <u>forced</u> to your knees...not because you wanted to, but because you <u>HAD</u> to. Because the thought of eating, drinking, or even going about life was not possible until you knew God had heard your plea on their behalf. Ask God to birth names in your thoughts that drive you between "the porch and the alter."

Will you pray for others right now?

Engage:

Grab a tissue, napkin, or paper towel and write out the names of those the Father brings to your mind on the tissue. It may be the names of people or specific situations. As you kneel place your face in the tissue representing that situation and desperately cry out to the Father. Embrace the joy of holy intervention.

Notes:

DAY 27

"The seed of God is in us. Given an intelligent and hard-working farmer, it will thrive and grow up to God, whose seed it is and accordingly its fruits will be God-nature"

- MEISTER ECKHART

Laban said to him, "Just because you are a relative of mine, should you work for me for nothing? Tell me what your wages should be."

Now Laban had two daughters; the name of the older was Leah, and the name of the younger was Rachel. Leah had weak eyes, but Rachel had a lovely figure and was beautiful. Jacob was in love with Rachel and said, "I'll work for you seven years in return for your younger daughter Rachel."

Laban said, "It's better that I give her to you than to some other man. Stay here with me." So Jacob served seven years to get Rachel, but they seemed like only a few days to him because of his love for her.

Then Jacob said to Laban, "Give me my wife. My time is completed, and I want to make love to her."

So Laban brought together all the people of the place and gave a feast. But when evening came, he took his daughter Leah and brought her to Jacob, and Jacob made love to her. And Laban gave his servant Zilpah to his daughter as her attendant.

When morning came, there was Leah! So Jacob said to Laban, "What is this you have done to me? I served you for Rachel, didn't I? Why have you deceived me?"

Laban replied, "It is not our custom here to give the younger daughter in marriage before the older one. Finish this daughter's bridal week; then we will give you the younger one also, in return for another seven years of work."

And Jacob did so. He finished the week with Leah, and then Laban gave him his daughter Rachel to be his wife. Laban gave his servant Bilhah to his daughter Rachel as her attendant. Jacob made love to Rachel also, and his love for Rachel was greater than his love for Leah. And he worked for Laban another seven years.

- Genesis 29:15-30

Read Genesis 29:15-30

Can you imagine?

Jacob, the deceiver, found himself deceived! Jacob, the one who once tricked his father for the reward of the firstborn though born second, unearthed an elaborate scheme devised to give away both daughters. There he sat, the swindler, having been swindled.

Jacob was placed right in the heart of a very difficult situation. Though a product reaping what had been sown, this new husband felt victimized and betrayed at the greatest level. The emotions he was experiencing, even though warranted, were very tangible. Leah was not the one for which he worked rigorously; Leah was not the one for which he gave seven years of labor; Leah was certainly not the one he intended to marry!

Read Galatians 6:7

It's a universal truth, applicable to both the spiritual and physical realm. One reaps what he/she sows. As one sows seeds of deception, they will reap the same. Hatred reaps hatred, kindness procures kindness. Seeds do not magically or supernaturally transform into other substances.

Seeds yield fruit of the same variety.

> *Quit expecting fruitful returns from seeds not sown.*

Reflect:

What have you been sowing lately?

Maybe you have felt betrayed; maybe you are the betrayer. Maybe your mind is filled with an intricate scheme bent on deceiving someone or maybe you have been the target of such a plot.

You alone determine what is sown from your own hands.

Engage:

Ask the Lord to reveal the seeds you have been sowing in the fields around you.

Repent of any areas where you have sown things not indicative of a son or daughter of the kingdom.

Ask the Father to reveal three areas where you can concentrate on sowing good seed today. If able, carry some seeds from your garden or fruit with you as a reminder of this precious truth.

Notes:

DAY 28

Do everything without grumbling or arguing.

- Philippians 2:14

Read Philippians 2:14

Some believers only appear to be happy when they are complaining. Others choose to "prayerfully" voice their grumbling and complaining. Griping has become so common among God's people it leaves many wondering if the church is a house of complaint or a house of prayer?

This is not new; however, the Israelites perfected this art long before we were ever born. They grew weary of food appearing on the ground, weary of the leadership God appointed, and weary of the land that had been delivered to them. Even in the middle of blessing, they often objected.

Oh, how we do the same thing!

One of the greatest testimonies of a follower of Christ is choosing joy over grumbling or complaining, a Divine perspective over a carnal substitute. We did not come to the cross to merely receive a ticket to heaven but also to transform our perspective regarding all of life. It is this heavenly perspective that allows us to shine amid darkness. After all, The King once rescued us from death bringing us into unspeakable joy and life.

> *When you are facing difficult circumstances or injustice, put on the lens of heaven and watch your complaints sink under the weight of His joy.*

Everyone grumbles and complains, right? *Complaining is a conscious choice not a mindless reaction!* According to Paul, complaining is a choice not some robot-like reaction to the stimuli of life. Our words and attitude can be a lifesaver in the ocean of complaints that constantly drown this world.

Reflect:

What areas of your life tend to make you grumble the most?

Where has your interaction with someone pointed to Christ or pulled people away from Christ?

Engage:

In the Notes Section list out the people, places, and things which you often allow to steal your joy when you choose to voice your complaints. Take some time to let the Holy Spirit reveal every area which is present. Now ask the Father to conquer these areas. Ask for the strength to choose joy over every possible complaint you could bring forth. Let the Holy Spirit speak into each area. As He does, intentionally and cheerfully mark through the inscription. After a time of celebration, thank the Father for the ability He gives to overcome.

Notes:

DAY 29

"Humility and love are precisely the graces which the men of the world can understand…. The poorest Christian can every day find occasion practicing love and humility"

- J. C. RYLE

Do nothing out of selfish ambition or vain conceit. Rather, in humility value others above yourselves, not looking to your own interests but each of you to the interests of the others.

In your relationships with one another, have the same mindset as Christ Jesus:

Who, being in very nature God, did not consider equality with God something to be used to his own advantage;
rather, he made himself nothing
by taking the very nature of a servant,
being made in human likeness.

And being found in appearance as a man,
he humbled himself
by becoming obedient to death—
even death on a cross!

Therefore God exalted him to the highest place
and gave him the name that is above every name,

that at the name of Jesus every knee should bow,
in heaven and on earth and under the earth,

and every tongue acknowledge that Jesus Christ is Lord,
to the glory of God the Father.

- Philippians 2:3-11

Read Philippians 2:3-11

This is indeed one of the greatest and yet most perplexing scriptures in the entirety of the Word. The Messiah and King consciously and intentionally chose to humble Himself. Stop and let this mind-blowing truth permeate your soul. King Jesus, the King of Kings and Lord of Lords, willingly and deliberately selected the limitations of becoming a servant instead of powerfully ruling over humanity. It certainly wasn't due to a lack of potential power. Blind eyes opened at his command, lepers' sores leapt off the skin they had cursed, and graves gave forth life at His very word. It most certainly was not a lack of power, but rather an act of intentional humility which ultimately led to His exaltation.

Humility in this sense was not the result of lowly circumstances but rather freedom from embracing arrogance, entitlement, or pride. Christ demonstrated his love and kindness by joyfully embracing the role evident within the pronouncement of the second chapter of Philippians. Scholars have labeled this section of scripture as the kenosis, or the self-emptying of Jesus. Paul eloquently recalls Jesus' humility to serve others and insists we have the same mind to serve one another.

> *As a Christ follower, our full-time profession is serving others.*

Reflect:

What would change in your relationships if you started having the same attitude as Jesus?

How can you tangibly imitate the humility of Jesus today?

Has pride, selfishness, or arrogance inhibited your relationships with one another?

Engage:

Choose to perform a selfless act for someone else today. Do not do it to be recognized or praised. Serve one another for the sake of the kingdom. Spend some time in prayer asking the Father to reveal someone you can serve. Whatever you find your hands to do, make sure to serve in a manner to promote the kingdom of Christ in others.

Notes:

DAY 30

"There is a loving God; He has spoken in the Bible. He means what He says and will do all He has promised"

- HUDSON TAYLOR

Just then a woman who had been subject to bleeding for twelve years came up behind him and touched the edge of his cloak. She said to herself, "If I only touch his cloak, I will be healed."

Jesus turned and saw her. "Take heart, daughter," he said, "your faith has healed you." And the woman was healed at that moment.

- Matthew 9:20-22

Read Matthew 9:20-22

She was desperate…truly desperate. She didn't just want God; she needed the Divine intervention of the King. There is a stark difference. She needed God to move so desperately she violently fell to her knees and crawled through the dirt…through the crowds…fighting her way through the masses. The depths of her need were marked by her relentless approach. Why?

This lady was not merely acting upon the suggestion or experience of others. She had a desperate need, but she also had something so incredible…something that gave her hope in the middle of chaos… Do not miss this… She had a *promise* from God.

There was a reason this lady touched the "hem" of his garment. This was not a mere stitch of clothing; the inclusion of this term has a much more distinct meaning than one can fathom. The "hem" was called the "wing" of a Jewish wardrobe. She wasn't just crawling and happened to touch the Messiah's garment. She purposefully acted upon a promise she heard read in the synagogues.

The Old Testament gloriously announces, "Healing was in the wings of the Messiah" (Malachi 4:2). When this afflicted woman fought through the crowds on her hands and feet she literally reached out and touched the "wings" of his garment. She placed her petition right on the promise she was holding on to…and the result was supernatural.

> ***Her petition and His promise gloriously collided!***

Reflect:

God faithfully honors His promises.

What about you? Is there something in your life that has you at a place of desperation, just like the woman in Matthew? Despair so challenging you need a promise to grasp tightly… a promise that brings hope… a promise that brings life… a promise from Someone able to keep their word who can directly affect your situation?

What petition / need do you have that needs to be placed directly on the guarantee of God?

In the notes section write out your requests to God.

Take some time to think over what you have written.

Engage:

It is one thing to bring a petition to the Lord; it is so much greater to bring your petition stamped with a Divine promise. What promise has God given you which gives you hope for your circumstance? Diligently search the scriptures for God's precious promises. Let the Holy Spirit guide you through each one you read.

Once you have been given a promise from the Lord, write it down.

Ask God to help you believe in the promise through prayer.

Notes:

DAY 31

"You're going to be a Christian, put everything that you've got to Christ, that's, your time, your talent, your everything."

- WILLIAM MARRION BRANHAM

"Again, it will be like a man going on a journey, who called his servants and entrusted his wealth to them. To one he gave five bags of gold, to another two bags, and to another one bag, each according to his ability. Then he went on his journey. The man who had received five bags of gold went at once and put his money to work and gained five bags more. So also, the one with two bags of gold gained two more. But the man who had received one bag went off, dug a hole in the ground and hid his master's money.

"After a long time the master of those servants returned and settled accounts with them. The man who had received five bags of gold brought the other five. 'Master,' he said, 'you entrusted me with five bags of gold. See, I have gained five more.'

"His master replied, 'Well done, good and faithful servant! You have been faithful with a few things; I will put you in charge of many things. Come and share your master's happiness!'

"The man with two bags of gold also came. 'Master,' he said, 'you entrusted me with two bags of gold; see, I have gained two more.'

"His master replied, 'Well done, good and faithful servant! You have been faithful with a few things; I will put you in charge of many things. Come and share your master's happiness!'

"Then the man who had received one bag of gold came. 'Master,' he said, 'I knew that you are a hard man, harvesting where you have not sown and

104

gathering where you have not scattered seed. So I was afraid and went out and hid your gold in the ground. See, here is what belongs to you.'

"His master replied, 'You wicked, lazy servant! So you knew that I harvest where I have not sown and gather where I have not scattered seed? Well then, you should have put my money on deposit with the bankers, so that when I returned I would have received it back with interest.

"So take the bag of gold from him and give it to the one who has ten bags. For whoever has will be given more, and they will have an abundance. Whoever does not have, even what they have will be taken from them. And throw that worthless servant outside, into the darkness, where there will be weeping and gnashing of teeth.'

- Matthew 25:14-30

Read Matthew 25:14-30

Do you ever look at someone and think, "Man if I had their size, or their speed, or their voice, or their smarts, or their talent, I'd be unstoppable?" Quite often we say these things about someone we feel hasn't used or lived according to their abilities given them. They haven't used their God given talents. But what about you? What are you doing with what God has given to you? I'm not talking about simply excelling on a sports field, business field, classroom, or concert hall. What are you doing with your "God given talents" for the kingdom?

Jesus often spoke in parables or stories to communicate a point to those listening. This particular story is known as the parable of talents. A talent referred to a measure of money, and while there are various interpretations of this specific parable, one thing is clear, Jesus expects us to do something with what we have been given.

In this parable, Jesus highlights those that are faithful with what they are given and contrasts them with those who have been lazy with what they have been entrusted. Two of the servants took the talent given them and used them to bring about an increase, while the third man in the parable did nothing with what he was given other than bury it. As a result, they are richly rewarded while he is harshly rebuked and punished.

In a Spiritual sense, the "talents" in this parable represent the things God has blessed you with to be used to further His kingdom – both natural abilities, acquired talents, and spiritual gifts. These may be literal "talents" such as speaking, singing, writing, encouragement etc. that we typically think of being used in a church or worship setting. Or maybe physical talents/gifts such as athletic ability or academic intelligence. Perhaps you've been blessed financially or you are a great listener or good with your hands.

> *Unfortunately, most believers nowadays simply do nothing.*

Reflect:

What has God given to you to be used to further the kingdom?

Ask God in prayer right now to reveal everything he has blessed you with to advance His kingdom. Take as much time as you need to let Him reveal it to you. As it is revealed, write it in the notes section of this page.

Engage:

Understanding what you been given is huge, but as we see from this parable, the ultimate goal is utilizing it in the kingdom.

The question is: What are you going to do with these talents you have been given?

Grab a coin and carry it with you all day. Don't merely mix it with other change, but keep it in a place where you will constantly be engaged by its presence. The coin you are holding in your hand represents the things God has freely and graciously given you. Ask the Lord to help you use everything He has given to you for His glory. Throughout the day take the coin out and ask the Holy Spirit to fully awaken you to the possibilities of the kingdom around you.

Notes:

DAY 32

"Subtle he needs must be, who could seduce Angels"

- JOHN MILTON

If we claim to be without sin, we deceive ourselves and the truth is not in us.

- 1 John 1:8

If you think you are standing firm, be careful that you don't fall! No temptation has overtaken you except what is common to mankind. And God is faithful; he will not let you be tempted beyond what you can bear. But when you are tempted, he will also provide a way out so that you can endure it.

- 1 Corinthians 10:12-13

Submit yourselves, then, to God. Resist the devil, and he will flee from you.

- James 4:7

Do not set foot on the path of the wicked
or walk in the way of evildoers.

Avoid it, do not travel on it;
turn from it and go on your way.

For they cannot rest until they do evil;
they are robbed of sleep till they make someone stumble.

They eat the bread of wickedness
and drink the wine of violence.

The path of the righteous is like the morning sun,
shining ever brighter till the full light of day.

But the way of the wicked is like deep darkness;
they do not know what makes them stumble.

My son, pay attention to what I say;
turn your ear to my words.

Do not let them out of your sight,
keep them within your heart;

for they are life to those who find them
and health to one's whole body.

- Proverbs 4:14-22

Read 1 John 1:8, 1 Corinthians 10:12-13, James 4:7, Proverbs 4:14-22,

It all started when we were young. There was this cookie, the one you really wanted, your favorite. While warm and fresh out of the oven, the scent seemed to eloquently call to your stomach like a master to his dog. And your mom... she had the audacity, the pure craziness, to leave it on the counter directly in front of you with strict instructions, "Do not touch." Really? I mean why would she leave it right in front of you? Cookies were made to be eaten, and well, they would only be warm for a select moment... maybe she wouldn't notice. After all, it's just one cookie, right? You get closer and the smell that permeated the room now grabs the attention of your nostrils in a way that renders you helpless. You take another step closer, and you see the chocolate chips have melted perfectly into the sugary dough. Yet another step and even your simple mathematical mind realizes there are plenty delicacies for everyone in the family to have at least two. Your mind begins this crazy game.... Mom won't care, it's just one cookie, and this is the most perfect moment in time to indulge. As you down the cookie, you hear the dreadful announcement from your mother. Of course, you lie, but she knows. The chocolate stains in between the cracks of your teeth have told a tale your words could not.

Temptation... it stinks doesn't it? As we get older the temptation changes from cookies to things of deeper emotional value: disobedience, spiritual laziness, sexual indulgence, prayerlessness, and much more.

Ever since the Garden of Eden, people have faced temptation. For Adam and Eve, it was the forbidden fruit. For us, it is a host of things. And for some reason, we do not flee from the temptation, we get closer and closer and closer and closer...until we can see the steam rising off the cookie.

> *Do not just resist the temptation, flee from it completely.*

Reflect:

What is the enemy dangling before you right now?

To what are you most vulnerable?

Maybe you've taken five steps forward and are gazing into the temptation with amazing accuracy.

What is it that hangs from the jagged teeth of a trap waiting to devour you spiritually?

What temptations are dangling before you like beautiful bright red apples right this moment.

Engage:

Make yourself your favorite dessert, a bowl of ice cream, warm chocolate chip cookies, or a slice of pie. Let it sit in front of you on the table. As it sits in front of you on the table, refuse to give in to it. Ask the Father to help you resist the temptation the enemy is dangling in front of you, not the dessert, the sin that waits at your door to devour you. After time in prayer, throw away the dessert without indulging. Use it as a victorious symbol of fleeing from the enemy's temporary desires which lead to death.

Notes:

Take a moment in prayer to ask the Father to help identify areas of temptation that are hanging before you. Seriously ask Him right now.

DAY 33

"All heaven is interested in the cross of Christ, all hell terribly afraid of it, while men are the only beings who more or less ignore its meaning."

- OSWALD CHAMBERS

This is why it is said:

"Wake up, sleeper,
rise from the dead,
and Christ will shine on you."

Be very careful, then, how you live—not as unwise but as wise, making the most of every opportunity, because the days are evil. Therefore do not be foolish, but understand what the Lord's will is.

- Ephesians 5:14-17

Now listen, you who say, "Today or tomorrow we will go to this or that city, spend a year there, carry on business and make money." Why, you do not even know what will happen tomorrow. What is your life? You are a mist that appears for a little while and then vanishes.

- James 4:13-14

Read Ephesians 5:14-17, James 4:13-14

There is such a thing as spiritual sleep. It is entirely possible to be physically present in all the places you are supposed to be yet still slumbering spiritually. You can even be doing the right things, saying the right things, singing the right songs, and miss it entirely.

This is a terrifying and dreadful thought. What if your activity looks good, but you are completely unaware of everything God is wanting to do because you are asleep? What if you are just going through the motions, performing religious activities, and missing what God has in store for you?

Have you ever found yourself spiritually asleep?

Notice Ephesians 5:14: "Wake up, O sleeper, rise from the dead." This verse is often spoken to sinners, but it was not written to sinners. Ephesians was never written to sinners. It is not a message to sinners at all, but a message to one of the best churches in the New Testament.

One of the greatest recorded revivals that ever occurred happened within the limits of the Ephesus church. Yet the writer says, "Wake up, O sleeper, rise from the dead, and Christ will shine on you."

It is perfectly possible for good, faithful, loyal people to be spiritually asleep—being in a spiritual state that parallels natural sleep. You must be awakened suddenly. Apathetic souls are sleepy souls. Do not, under any circumstance, continue in your spiritual sleep.

> *The most pressing obligation of the apathetic is to wake up.*

113

Reflect:

What is it God is calling you to do right now?

What do you need to wake up to in your own life?

God hasn't redeemed you merely to sit and wait for heaven one day. God is speaking, and wants to reveal Himself to you and me, but most of us are so asleep, unconscious, and unable to hear Him.

Engage:

What do you do to wake up on time? Grab your phone and set at least 7 alarms to go off during your day today. As each alarm goes off, stop whatever you are doing and ask the Father to awaken you from the slumber of a normal life. After your petition, spend some time letting Christ shine upon you with his presence.

Notes:

DAY 34

"Oh, how great peace and quietness would he possess who should cut off all vain anxiety and place all his confidence in God"

- THOMAS A KEMPIS

Humble yourselves, therefore, under God's mighty hand, that he may lift you up in due time. Cast all your anxiety on him because he cares for you.

Be alert and of sober mind. Your enemy the devil prowls around like a roaring lion looking for someone to devour. Resist him, standing firm in the faith, because you know that the family of believers throughout the world is undergoing the same kind of sufferings.

And the God of all grace, who called you to his eternal glory in Christ, after you have suffered a little while, will himself restore you and make you strong, firm and steadfast. To him be the power for ever and ever. Amen.

- 1 Peter 5:6-11

Read 1 Peter 5:6-11

"Sober-minded" …that sounds nice, doesn't it? But who in the world can be sober minded in such a world as the one we live in? You can!

With the treacherous volumes of tasks we navigate during the day and the schedule we must keep – is this really possible? It is!

Anxiety appears to be the farthest thing from being sober-minded, and it also seems to be the epidemic of our generation. In the last decade, anxiety has overtaken depression as the number one reason people in the United States seek counseling. Our minds and schedules have become so busy, we are addicted to the anxiety to which we have grown so accustomed.

> *If you are a person marked by anxiety, it's*
> *ok to not be ok...*
> *but you do not have to remain in such a*
> *demanding and vile state!*

Being sober-minded doesn't mean my schedule is free; it simply means I am free from the intoxicating influences that would rob me of thinking clearly. In other words, my mind is not clouded with thoughts of anxiety, depression, and fear but with the freedom and hope I have from being a child of God. A sober mind is a mind set on the things of Christ, the things of eternity. This eternal perspective conquers all our momentary fears and worries.

Reflect:

What are you allowing to cloud your thinking?

What are you anxious about?

Where are you allowing temporary trials to steal the joy of having an eternal perspective?

How can you humble yourself before the mighty hand of God in this very moment?

Engage:

Create a thought log. Journal how and where you give your minds attention during a normal day / week. Prayerfully look over the list and allow the Holy Spirit to help you eliminate portions of the list which are debilitating to walking sober-minded. As you evaluate each portion, ask the question, "Where is God in this?" Have I taken on good things to fill my schedule instead of prayerfully submitting them to God?". After going through the list, pray and commit to intentionally making each activity about glorifying Christ.

Notes:

DAY 35

Now the king of Aram was at war with Israel. After conferring with his officers, he said, "I will set up my camp in such and such a place."

The man of God sent word to the king of Israel: "Beware of passing that place, because the Arameans are going down there." So the king of Israel checked on the place indicated by the man of God. Time and again Elisha warned the king, so that he was on his guard in such places.

This enraged the king of Aram. He summoned his officers and demanded of them, "Tell me! Which of us is on the side of the king of Israel?"

"None of us, my lord the king," said one of his officers, "but Elisha, the prophet who is in Israel, tells the king of Israel the very words you speak in your bedroom."

"Go, find out where he is," the king ordered, "so I can send men and capture him." The report came back: "He is in Dothan." [14] Then he sent horses and chariots and a strong force there. They went by night and surrounded the city.

When the servant of the man of God got up and went out early the next morning, an army with horses and chariots had surrounded the city. "Oh no, my lord! What shall we do?" the servant asked.

"Don't be afraid," the prophet answered. "Those who are with us are more than those who are with them."

And Elisha prayed, "Open his eyes, Lord, so that he may see." Then the Lord opened the servant's eyes, and he looked and saw the hills full of horses and chariots of fire all around Elisha.

As the enemy came down toward him, Elisha prayed to the Lord, "Strike this army with blindness." So he struck them with blindness, as Elisha had asked.

Elisha told them, "This is not the road and this is not the city. Follow me, and I will lead you to the man you are looking for." And he led them to Samaria.

- 2 Kings 6:8-19

Read 2 Kings 6: 8-19

Beyond a doubt, this is many Christ followers' favorite passage of scripture. It overflows with the heart of God and screams of the reality of things unseen. It makes us increasingly aware of the kingdom we are a part of as Christians and reminds us of the overwhelming power of God. Why? Though we may feel we are all alone, God has completely and powerfully surrounded us. This theme seems to be repeated all throughout scripture.

Daniel knew he would not be alone when he was served up as food to hungry lions.

Hananiah, Mishael, and Azariah had confidence their God would be with them even in the burning embers of the fiery furnace.

David cried out multiple times knowing that God was able to rescue him from being alone.

Elijah cried out to God and said he was all alone, but God reassured him there were hundreds that were still pure.

This passage was not simply recorded so we could have a cool story to talk about. It happened… and guess what? God is still as present, actually even closer, than ever before.

We are made aware of it all through the scriptures. God will not leave us alone. Hebrews tells us that we have Jesus constantly interceding for us. Christ left his disciples with a word of comfort not of despair. Jesus told his followers that it was better for Him to leave so the Comforter may come.

> ### *We are most certainly not alone.*

Reflect:

You may feel all alone in your life right now. You may feel like there is darkness all around you. Not sinful, self-induced darkness, but the darkness which comes because of the enemy's lies as they penetrate your thinking. As he deceivingly utters, "No one cares about you," "You are the only one left," "No one will even notice." No matter what you are going through, the King of Kings, the Lord of Lords, our great and Mighty warrior, our Savior, Our Redeemer, the One who speaks life into existence, Who performs miracles, Who battles for us...HE IS WITH YOU!

Just like those that have come before us, we need an ever present very near God. But do not be deceived, we do, in fact, have an ever present very near God.

Engage:

Write the words "Not Alone" on a piece of paper and place it in your pocket for the day. Pull it out occasionally and ask the Lord to open your eyes to the overwhelming reality of His nearness.

Notes:

DAY 36

"God will not be used as a convenience. Men or nations who think they can revive the Faith in order to make a good society might just as well think they can use the stairs of heaven as a shortcut to the nearest chemist's shop"

- C.S. LEWIS

After this he went down to Capernaum with his mother and brothers and his disciples. There they stayed for a few days.

Jesus Clears the Temple Courts

When it was almost time for the Jewish Passover, Jesus went up to Jerusalem. In the temple courts he found people selling cattle, sheep and doves, and others sitting at tables exchanging money. So he made a whip out of cords, and drove all from the temple courts, both sheep and cattle; he scattered the coins of the money changers and overturned their tables. To those who sold doves he said, "Get these out of here! Stop turning my Father's house into a market!" His disciples remembered that it is written: "Zeal for your house will consume me."

- John 2:12-17

Read John 2:12-17

Wait, what just happened? Did Jesus just do what I think He did? This along with the other gospel accounts are some of the most intense conflicts surrounding Jesus' ministry. If anyone ever tells you that Jesus wasn't controversial, they haven't read the Bible! Jesus goes to the temple, sees what is transpiring, and is intensely filled with a desire to stop the repulsive things occurring there. Most of the time, we picture Jesus as this Precious Moments figurine just going around and loving on everyone, when in actuality, He was one of the most controversial persons ever to walk the face of the earth. Jesus grabs a whip and drives all the sacrificial animals from the temple, while turning over tables, and throwing the exchange money on the ground. Can you imagine?

Why in the world did the Messiah do this? The scriptures say the people in the temple were selling sheep, cattle, and doves. It is very interesting that those are the very things used in the sacrificial system. Without some understanding of the Old Testament, you may miss what is going on here and just assume Jesus had a strange style of worship.

Before the crucifixion of Jesus, followers of God would go to the temple and make offerings for their sin. When the temple was first built, they had just seen God supernaturally intervene in their lives. As a result, they graciously poured out their sacrifices to Him. They were instructed to bring animals which were without blemish and the best of their entire livestock. After all, you do not bring your worst as an offering to the King of Kings. As time progressed however, people became lazy and brought less than their best. Instead of bringing their own animals for sacrifice, they would go to people who had tables at the temple where worshipers could simply just buy the animals they needed.

Do you see what was going on? Instead of willingly and lovingly bringing a sacrifice to God, they were doing what they thought they could get by with and merely going through the motions.

> *They were making church as convenient as possible while having as little sacrifice as they could.*

Sound familiar? I cannot even begin to express how much this sounds like modern American Christianity. While we may not be buying sacrificial animals at church, we do the least amount possible for the kingdom, lest we suffer loss. This is King Jesus we are talking about! He is worthy of the very best effort, the very best of our possessions, the very best of our time, and the very best of everything we have to offer. After all, when it came to intervening on our behalf, Jesus gave His very life. How insulting it must be for Him to look on us bringing anything less than our best.

Jesus isn't some charity-case; He is our King! How could we be content to bring anything less that absolutely everything?

Don't be deceived. We don't give our best for Him to be pleased with us...and we certainly don't give our best to try to earn anything. If the level of our commitment determined how we received the favor of God, we would all be in trouble. We give our best because He deserves it. He deserves all that you have, or ever will have. HE IS THAT GOOD! The problem isn't necessarily just the sacrifice; it's that we have forgotten how incredible our King really is.

Reflect:

Look around the room and spend some time asking yourself where you have been giving less than what He deserves.

Where have you been choosing convenience over commitment?

What tables do you need to throw over in your own life? Be honest.

Engage:

Turn something upside down in your home… a chair, some decoration, or familiar piece. Leave the piece upside down the entire day. Approach the Father in prayer, creating an open invitation to turn over whatever he needs to in order to align your life with His will. Confess your shortcomings, and let Jesus drive out anything not pleasing to the King.

Notes:

DAY 37

*"Revenge... is like a rolling stone, which, when a man hath
forced up a hill, will return upon him with a greater violence,
and break those bones whose sinews gave it motion"*

- A L B E R T   S C H W E I T Z E R

Saul told his son Jonathan and all the attendants to kill David. But Jonathan had taken a great liking to David.

- 1 Samuel 19:1

Saul tried to pin him to the wall with his spear, but David eluded him as Saul drove the spear into the wall. That night David made good his escape.

Saul sent men to David's house to watch it and to kill him in the morning. But Michal, David's wife, warned him, "If you don't run for your life tonight, tomorrow you'll be killed." So Michal let David down through a window, and he fled and escaped. Then Michal took an idol and laid it on the bed, covering it with a garment and putting some goats' hair at the head.

When Saul sent the men to capture David, Michal said, "He is ill."

- 1 Samuel 19:10-14

Read 1 Samuel 19:1,10-14

When Saul misses, David has a grueling decision. The Bible describes the scene where Saul hurls his spear at David, and it sticks in the wall directly beside him. At this point, David has a choice to make: Does he respond in the same manner by violently heaving the blade towards Saul or was an alternative response more pleasing to God?

As a human our natural tendency is to strike back, to bite when bitten. David wasn't just capable of striking back; he was skilled beyond measure. Ask Goliath about David's aim. If you're going to throw a spear at David, you better not miss. But David does what must have been the most challenging thing he ever did...nothing.

> *In moments of offense, the hardest thing to do is nothing at all.*

This isn't the only time David could have killed Saul. Read the account in 1 Samuel 24:1-12, 1 Samuel 26:7-10. Even after David suffered greatly from Saul's hand, even after David could have justifiably killed Saul, even though Saul was committing kingly resources to try and kill David... David still chose *not* to take things into his own hands!

It wasn't that David was a coward; he had faced giants. It wasn't that he lacked the capability to kill Saul; David had conquered more than Saul ever did. David had confidence the same hand that had plucked him from the sheep field and the same hand that had delivered him from lions and bears and Goliaths could deliver him from all situations.

David realized a great truth that would forever stay with Him – The King is much better at fighting battles than he is!

Reflect:

Is there someone who has done things to wrong you or hurt you? Maybe they have said something about you or betrayed you. Inwardly, you have the desire to just "get even" or "make them pay". Ask the Father to help you respond positively towards that person instead of seeking revenge.

You may not have anyone throwing spears at you, but what situation do you need to hand over to the Lord, to trust him more?

What "spears" have been thrown at you? Who has thrown those "spears"? What battle is raging in your life?

What have you taken into your hands instead of letting the King fight for you?

What battle has left you tired and fruitless? Maybe you've even made a mess of things.

Who do you need to extend grace to instead of hurling a spear back in their direction?

Spend some time and let the Lord reveal them to you right now before continuing...

As hard as it seems and contrary to our human nature, the scriptures tell us in Matthew 5:44 to "Love our enemies and pray for those who persecute you." Wow. This is not a normal worldly response. The best part is

FREEDOM comes as a result.

Engage:

Take some time to let the Lord prepare your heart regarding *that* person and *that* situation. You know the situation. The one that you don't want to talk about, the one which surfaces all kinds of hidden emotions. Ask the Lord to heal your heart regarding the situation. Now, use the note section to write out a prayer for the offender. Genuinely intercede for them. Ask for the Father to reveal Himself in ways divine. Close by humbly voicing the prayer to your King.

Notes:

DAY 38

"The natural role of twentieth-century man is anxiety"

- NORMAN MAILER

Rejoice in the Lord always. I will say it again: Rejoice! Let your gentleness be evident to all. The Lord is near. Do not be anxious about anything, but in every situation, by prayer and petition, with thanksgiving, present your requests to God. And the peace of God, which transcends all understanding, will guard your hearts and your minds in Christ Jesus.

- Philippians 4:4-7

Read Philippians 4:4-7

One of the greatest treasures found in the scriptures surfaces in the last chapter of Philippians. Within these small verses is a promise that quickens the Spirit of all believers across cultures, socioeconomic status, and levels of maturity.

Do you often find yourselves worrying to the level of producing anxiety? Do you find yourself in a constant state of fret to the point of restless nights, depression, and unrest?

Anxious people are often prayerless people!

When anxiety is reigning in the life of a believer, the peace of God seems to be as distant as the east from the west. Paul however states the peace of God, which passes all understanding, will guard your hearts and minds in Christ Jesus. Paul does not say, "it may" or "for 1 in 10" ...no. Paul's encouragement is Divine peace which will flow when there is prayer, supplication, and thanksgiving before the Lord. It is unfortunate so many continue diligently searching for peace that is so readily available through Jesus.

Though we often label anxiety as the epidemic of our time, it has plagued mankind since its existence. While writing from a jail cell with the uncertain threat of possible death, Paul thought it necessary to admonish other believers not to be anxious about anything. Find the joy of letting peace replace your anxiety.

Reflect:

What is it you are finding yourself anxious about?

Are there relationships in your life that lead to high levels of anxiety?

What false expectations do you have which are fueling anxiety?

Engage:

Make a list of the current anxieties plaguing you. Write them down in the Notes section.

After a time of reflection, lift your anxieties to the King who has authority over all your circumstances reaching even within the foundations of your very mind. As you prayerfully reflect over each, allow the Father to supernaturally speak into these areas individually.

Notes:

DAY 39

*"God never ceases to speak to us, but the noise of the world
without and the tumult of our passions within bewilder us and
prevent us from listening to Him"*

- F. FENELON

My sheep listen to my voice; I know them, and they follow me.

- John 10:27

So I say, walk by the Spirit, and you will not gratify the desires of the
flesh.

- Galatians 5:16

For what the law was powerless to do because it was weakened by the
flesh, God did by sending his own Son in the likeness of sinful flesh to be
a sin offering. And so he condemned sin in the flesh, in order that the
righteous requirement of the law might be fully met in us, who do not live
according to the flesh but according to the Spirit.

Those who live according to the flesh have their minds set on what the
flesh desires; but those who live in accordance with the Spirit have their
minds set on what the Spirit desires.

- Romans 8:3-5

Do not get drunk on wine, which leads to debauchery. Instead, be filled
with the Spirit,

- Ephesians 5:18

Read John 10:27, Galatians 5:16, Romans 8:3-5, Ephesians 5:18

We used to play a game when we were younger called "Simon Says". You most likely played it as well. It was a fast pace and somewhat intense game for someone below the age of 7. One person gives commands, tells you what to do, and you are supposed to respond. The kicker is you are only supposed to respond when you hear the words "Simon says" prior to the command. For children with listening issues, this game can often be a very frustrating exercise in listening skills.

As we get older, we abandon the child like games of "Simon Says" and migrate on to bigger and more mature decisions. It appears that many of us, like little children, have poor listening skills when it comes to following the Holy Spirit.

Do you know the voice of God? Can you distinguish between the voice of the Father and everything else going on around you? Like little children playing a game of "Simon Says", it is sometimes difficult to know when to move and what to do. The Father speaks in a variety of ways personal to each person.

How do you recognize the voice of God?

One thing is sure, people have asked this question throughout all recorded time. There are even chronicled events in the Bible of those who struggled to know what He sounded like (Samuel). Thankfully, we already have the revelation of God recorded in the holy scriptures, but we have also been endowed with the Holy Spirit which breathes new life in our circumstances.

Reflect:

Most of us have grown too busy, too loud, to hear the Lord, to really focus on his voice. We rush from event to event, responsibility to responsibility, and we miss His leading moment by moment. The noise of busyness can deafen the still small voice of the Savior. Do not confuse motion with activity.

> ### *There is such a thing as sacred idleness.*

Engage:

Read Psalm 46:10.

Read the passage and take some time to reflect. When was the last time you were still, truly still. Take this moment right now, to stop and listen for His voice. Ask the Father for a "Simon Says" moment... directions that you can respond to.

Wait for Him!

Be Still!

Listen!

As the Father reveals Himself, record it in the Notes section.

Notes:

DAY 40

The earth is the Lord's, and everything in it,
the world, and all who live in it;

for he founded it on the seas
and established it on the waters.

Who may ascend the mountain of the Lord?
Who may stand in his holy place?

The one who has clean hands and a pure heart,
who does not trust in an idol

or swear by a false god.
They will receive blessing from the Lord
and vindication from God their Savior.

Such is the generation of those who seek him,
who seek your face, God of Jacob.

Lift up your heads, you gates;
be lifted up, you ancient doors,
that the King of glory may come in.

Who is this King of glory?
The Lord strong and mighty,
the Lord mighty in battle.

Lift up your heads, you gates;
lift them up, you ancient doors,
that the King of glory may come in.

Who is he, this King of glory?
The Lord Almighty—
he is the King of glory.

- Psalm 24

Come near to God and he will come near to you. Wash your hands, you sinners, and purify your hearts, you double-minded.

- James 4:8

Read Psalm 24 and James 4:8

There were a lot of things that filled my mind when our first child was born. I was nervous, scared, excited, and filled with a host of other emotions. There were so many things going on that were completely foreign to me. I quietly watched the doctors with anticipation and wonder. Though there were many things that baffled me, one thing stood out, and it was a common task.

They were washing their hands. Again, and again, and again, not just to their wrists but all the way up to their elbows. With frothy bands of white soap, they were almost choking amidst the suds. How can you wash your hands this feverishly and not chap them to dust? I had never seen anyone wash up like this. I had also never washed my hands like the medical staff. Never had I spent that much energy and attention in cleansing all the dirtiness of my day from my arms. I merely placed a small blot of soap on my hands and gently rubbed them together while thinking about what I was going to do next. They were meticulous, sure to cleanse off everything that could potentially contaminate themselves or someone else.

In the middle of everything else going on, I was reminded of the words of James "Draw nigh to God, and he will draw nigh to you. Cleanse your hands, ye sinners; and purify your hearts, ye double minded."

When it comes to our sins, I think many of us merely dab a little bit of soap on a small portion of our lives; we don't meticulously cleanse everything to rid ourselves of the contamination.

We are dirty…like really dirty!

Imagine the ghastly state of our physical bodies if they indicated our inward sinfulness.

We would be unrecognizably filthy! There are many things in our lives that our Father must conquer to make us pure before Him.

Reflect:

I know it's not fun, but take some time to think on your sin—the dirt in your life. Allow the Father to shine a light on even the darkest parts of your life.

What is it that continually surfaces in your life?

What is it that continually leads you to separation from our Savior? Pray and ask God to reveal your sin to you. Take as long as you need.

Engage:

After the Lord reveals your sin, grab a pen from around your house. Write out words or symbols of your sin on your hands. Write everything the Lord reveals, even if it is all over your hand. Take some time to look at your hands, to see how dirty your hands are before the Lord. There is good news. Through Jesus, your hands can become clean. Ask the Lord to cleanse you of your sin, to help you overcome the dirt in your life, and to give you clean hands. Pray, ask for grace, repent. As a symbol of Christ's forgiveness washing over you, go to a sink and wash your hands thoroughly, removing all signs of what was written.

Notes:

Made in the USA
Monee, IL
27 September 2024